SOUTH-WESTE

# HUMAN RELATIONS at work

**STEVEN A. EGGLAND, PH.D.**
Professor of Vocational and Adult Education
The University of Nebraska
Lincoln, Nebraska

**JOHN W. WILLIAMS, PH.D.**
U S WEST Communications
Denver, Colorado

SOUTH-WESTERN PUBLISHING CO.

FOURTH EDITION

**Credits:**
*Senior Acquisitions Editor:* Eve Lewis
*Senior Developmental Editor:* Willis S. Vincent
*Production Editor:* Karen E. Davis
*Associate Director/Design:* Darren K. Wright
*Associate Photo Editor/Stylist:* Fred M. Middendorf
*Associate Director/Photography:* Diana W. Fleming
*Assistant Photographer:* Mimi Ostendorf
*Marketing Manager:* Donald H. Fox
*Cartoons:* Carl Kock, Chicago, IL
*Cover Illustration:* Beth Mathes



ISBN: 0-538-61092-1

Library of Congress Catalog Card Number:
91-62594

2 3 4 5 6 DH 97 96 95 94 93

Printed in the United States of America

# Preface

The fourth edition of *Human Relations at Work* is written for and about people who are beginning their work-life. This text-workbook is based on empirically derived competencies that apply to all employees—whether they work for businesses, governmental units, or nonprofit institutions such as hospitals and schools.

Like the three very successful previous editions, the 4th Edition of *Human Relations at Work* is written in such a way as to be simple to read and easy to understand. It has translated the sophisticated terminology and concepts of social psychology into everyday language to which students can readily relate. Since the human relations movement also contains a great deal of "trendy" language that tends to lack endurance, this vocabulary, too, is avoided in the text.

## Revision Highlights

*Human Relations at Work,* 4th Edition, derives its strength from the suggestions of teachers and students who have used the first three editions. The significant changes include:

1. Chapter One has had a great deal of material added that deals with the timely topic of total quality management of personnel. This chapter also contains some new material covering laws that effect human relations in the workplace, such as those dealing with employees' health and security.
2. Chapter Three has been reoriented and now looks at human relations with fellow employees from the perspective of teamwork.
3. Chapter Four includes new material about leadership; specifically coaching and mentoring.
4. Several new activities have been added to the various chapters and improvements have been made on the existing activities.

As with the 3rd Edition, the 4th Edition is accompanied by a module on class activities (Stock No. GK30DD) drawn from the text-workbook. The module is available for teachers who wish to have the additional flexibility of using only certain materials for shorter time periods of instruction.

## Organization of the Text-Workbook

The text-workbook is divided into six chapters appearing in a very logical sequence. The first chapter develops an understanding of and an appreciation for human relations, including a discussion of equal employment opportunity and affirmative action. The second chapter is devoted to the most important first step in the development of human relations competencies—an improvement of the self concept and an understanding of oneself. The third, fourth, and fifth chapters deal with the three most important groups or populations with which people at work must deal. They are co-workers, employers, and customers. They are entitled Teamwork, Organizational Effectiveness, and Customer Focus, respectively. The final chapter develops, in the manner of a summary, the obvious link between human relations skills and communications skills. It is entitled Interpersonal Communication.

Throughout the text (at the end of each chapter) are dozens of class activities that, like the rest of the text, are appropriate for all secondary school students. The activities are designed to provide realistic and participative experiences that will help to develop the concepts brought out in the chapters. Because of the nature of human relations, most of the activities involve group work and group interaction. The teacher is encouraged to be flexible, creative, and inventive when assigning or directing the student activities. Suggestions for expanded and additional activities are found in the Teacher's Manual (GK30DX). The text has been specifically designed to cover all of the new basic skills in the human relations realm. In addition, many and various concepts associated with communicating at work are presented.

## Various Ways to Use This Text-Workbook

Finally, this text-workbook may be used in a great variety of settings and over varying lengths of time. It will be absolutely appropriate in virtually any vocational education class. The text is written to be appropriate for students from ninth grade and up. The time consumed could range from six weeks to a full semester, or it could be a part of another class or become a class in itself. Its use will depend on the professional teacher's analysis of students' needs. However, and for whatever use is made of this publication, it is the authors' sincere wish that it contributes specifically to a pluralistic work force and to the development of greater human relations skills among students preparing for employment and, more generally, to greater tolerance and understanding among people.

**S.A.E.**
**J.W.W.**

# Contents

# Chapter 1
# Understanding Human Relations

KNOWLEDGE: After reading this chapter, you will be able to:

1. Define *human relations.*
2. Describe four aspects of human relations as related to oneself, co-workers, customers, and supervisors.
3. Compare and contrast management's view of human relations today and in the early 1900s.
4. Distinguish between equal employment policies and affirmative-action programs.
5. Identify four laws that support equal employment opportunity.
6. Identify six common affirmative-action requirements.
7. Describe why employers want good human relations between employees and themselves.
8. Explain the relationship between technical knowledge and people knowledge.
9. Explain the meaning of gaining a competitive advantage through people.
10. Describe how good human relations enables a person to succeed at work.

ATTITUDES: After reading this chapter, you will:

1. Appreciate the relationship between technical knowledge and people knowledge.
2. Understand that employers want good human relations between employees and themselves.
3. Believe that success at work is dependent on good human relations.
4. Agree that practicing good human relations will result in a higher quality of worklife.

Learning about human relations as a participant may be the most interesting and exciting activity you've ever experienced. You will soon discover that dealing effectively with people is as simple as understanding a few basic concepts. But it can be more complex than nuclear physics or computer technology. This book will get you started on a fascinating trip on the way to finding out how to get along with others, especially at work.

To understand human relations, first you must know what it is. Then you must know why human relations is important. This beginning chapter helps you with these concepts and also includes a brief history of the development of human relations. Read and study this chapter carefully, and then complete the Activities at the end of the chapter. These Activities will increase your preliminary understanding of human relations.

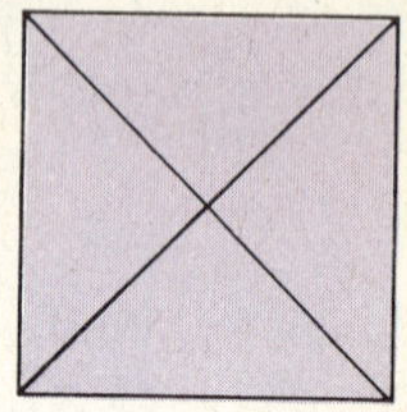


Illus. 1-1. Human relationships at work.

## THE NATURE OF HUMAN RELATIONS AT WORK

The term human relations refers to relationships between people. These relationships can be formal or informal, close or distant, emotional or unemotional. At work many kinds of relationships with different people must be considered. As an employee of a business, for example, you have relationships with yourself, your co-workers, your supervisor, and customers of the business. These relationships at work are illustrated by the square in Illus. 1-1.

### Your Relationship with Yourself

The study of human relations must begin with a study of yourself. "That's silly," you might say, "How can I have a relationship with myself?" The answer, of course, is not that you really have a relationship with yourself. Rather, it means that you get to know and like yourself. You learn to accept yourself for what you are. This is important to do before you develop good relationships with others.

You can only relate positively and successfully to others if you know yourself and feel good about yourself. If you don't know yourself very well and don't like yourself, this will be very obvious to others. For example, if you are inconsistent, nervous, self-conscious, and unpredictable, people will have difficulty knowing how to react to you. In other words, they will neither be able to relate to you very well nor have a good relationship with you. Chapter 2 will help you learn to understand and like yourself.

### Relationships with Co-Workers

As an employee you will spend a great deal of time with your co-workers. There are many reasons why it is important to get along with them. Your co-workers may help you or hinder your work. If you learn to get along with them, they will support you and help you to get through the rough spots of employment. If you do

Illus. 1-2. Get to know and like yourself.

not get along with them, you can expect very little cooperation from them.

There are several techniques you can master that will improve your relationships with co-workers. Learning to be accepted, carrying your own weight, and understanding unwritten and written rules are just a few of them. Chapter 3 will help you to be a team player.

## Relationships with Supervisors or Employers

The importance of learning to get along with a supervisor or employer can be easily seen. It can mean the difference between continued employment and termination. Learning how to better understand the supervisor and what that person expects of you is the key to a good relationship with an employer.

Illus. 1-3. Teamwork pays off.

Another way to improve your relationship with your employer is to try to put yourself in your employer's place. Imagining what it would be like to be an employer is a valuable tool that improves human relations with employers. Chapter 4 will give you practice in developing the skill of getting along with employers.

## Relationships with Customers

Most businesses operate under the rule that "the customer is always right." This rule is not to be taken literally but, rather, in spirit. Although the customer is not always right, the customer is always given the benefit of the doubt. The customer must be treated courteously and with respect. When customers or clients of a business are treated this way, the business and all its employees usually turn out to be successful.

Illus. 1-4. A customer focus is important to business.

It pays for a firm to develop positive and pleasant human relations with its customers because they will repeatedly return to the business. Employees of the business can help this to happen by developing good human relations with the customers. Chapter 5 will help you acquire the skill of getting along well with customers.

## IMPORTANCE OF HUMAN RELATIONS

Employers and managers have not always recognized the importance of human relations. During the first third of this century (1900–1930s), they saw little value in human relations. Employees were not treated very well. In those days most employers believed that employees:

1. Had little ambition and tended to shun work.
2. Actually disliked work and, when possible, tried to avoid it.
3. Were motivated by money only.[1]

### Beginning of the Human Relations Movement

The human relations movement actually began by accident. In the early 1930s, employers were conducting experiments to find ways of increasing the production of goods. One of these experiments, conducted at a Western Electric factory, produced some surprising results. It was this experiment that marked the beginning of the human relations movement.

#### *The Western Electric Experiment*

The purpose of the Western Electric experiment was to see if the amount of lighting in the factory affected the level of production. That is, the experimenters wanted to know if an increase in the amount of lighting would cause an increase in the production of telephone parts. It was hoped, of course, that better lighting would improve the quality and quantity of telephone parts being produced. To test this idea, the experimenters worked with the wiring department of the factory and installed special lights. After the special lights were installed, production of telephone parts increased.

---

1Douglas McGregor, *The Human Side of Enterprise* (New York: McGraw-Hill Book Company, 1960), pp. 33–34.

Illus. 1-5. Employers' views about employees early in this century.

The experimenters were naturally pleased with the results. They thought that the improved lighting had improved production.

A second part of this experiment called for decreasing the amount of lighting. The experimenters thought that if more light improved production, then less light would decrease production. To everyone's surprise, however, the workers continued to produce large amounts of high-quality parts even when the lighting was decreased. And when the lighting was returned to normal, the employees continued to work hard to increase production. As long as the experiment continued, the workers produced greater amounts of high-quality parts. When the experiment ended, the experimenters left the factory in a somewhat confused state because they did not expect these results. A few weeks later, however, production in the wiring department returned to the same level it was *before* the experiment was begun.

### *The Significance of the Western Electric Experiment*

The return to normal production had special meaning for the managers of the Western Electric plant. They realized that the experiment itself did not cause the increase in production. Rather, the reason for the increase in production was that the employees in the wiring department received special treatment while the experiment was being conducted. (The special treatment they received wasn't anything special by today's standards, but in those days it was.) The employees received special treatment because they were a part of the experiment. As a result of this special treatment, the employees believed that the owners of the business cared about them. Prior to the experiment, the owners' main interest in the employees was to make sure they worked. After the experiment ended, the employees felt that the owners were no longer interested in them. And that is when their production returned to the old level.

### *Effects of the Western Electric Experiment on Employers*

The news of the Western Electric experiment spread quickly. Alert business owners began to give employees more attention and recognition for their efforts. When employees were asked for their opinions on production problems, employers found that company goals were being reached more easily. The new emphasis at work was now on the employees. Their thoughts and feelings were becoming important. Because of the Western Electric experiment, a new era began in the management of employees. It was called the human relations movement.

## The Development of the Human Relations Movement

The human relations movement advanced slowly. Some years after the Western Electric experiment, employers became aware of the potential of employees. Employers began to recognize that employees were capable and eager to accept responsibility and wished to share in decision making. More recently, employers started to recognize prejudicial discrimination patterns in the employment of women, minorities, the handicapped, and older people. Actions taken with regard to these groups of people are creating a work environment free of unfair discrimination.

### *Meeting the Needs of Employees*

During the 1940s and the 1950s, more research similar to the Western Electric experiment was completed. Many activities that are common in organizations today are a result of this research. Such activities include: small-group problem solving, shared decision making, employee recognition programs, and management by objectives. The immediate results that employees of the 1950s realized were: better working conditions, retirement and benefit plans, and, most important, recognition of employees. Employers began to recognize their employees as a valuable resource for productive ideas.

By the end of the decade of the 1950s, most employers believed that:

1. If working conditions are favorable, most employees will not only accept responsibility, but also seek it.
2. The intellectual potential of the average employee is not being fully utilized by management.
3. When employees are committed to a company, they will exercise self-direction and self-control.

### *Equal Employment Opportunity and Affirmative Action*

Human relations in the 1960s marked the beginning of modern efforts to end prejudicial employment discrimination by treating all employees fairly. These efforts are referred to as *equal employment opportunity* and *affirmative action.*

Equal employment opportunity means that the personnel activities of an organization are conducted without prejudicial discrimination. Personnel activities include:

1. Recruiting and hiring.
2. Working conditions.
3. Salary, benefits, and privileges.

4. Training.
5. Promotions, downgrades, transfers, and layoffs.
6. Terminations.

Any discrimination between employees must result *because of lack of ability* and *not because* of race, color, religion, national origin, sex, age, or physical or mental handicap.

In addition to an organization's equal employment policies, the laws of the United States enacted by the federal government include the following acts:

1. Equal Pay Act (1963). This act requires employers to give employees equal pay for equal work.
2. Civil Rights Act, Title VII (1964). Title VII prohibits discrimination on the basis of race, sex, religion, or national origin.
3. Age Discrimination in Employment Act (1967). This act prohibits discrimination in personnel activities because of age.
4. The Americans Disabilities Act (1991). This act is a broad prohibition of discrimination on the basis of disability. The term *disability* means a physical or mental impairment that substantially limits one or more of the major life activities of an individual.

Affirmative action is literally a positive movement toward a prejudice-free work environment. An organization which

Illus. 1-6. The human relations movement is working toward eliminating prejudicial employment discrimination.

states that it is an affirmative-action employer has an ongoing program that guarantees equal opportunity for all employees.

Affirmative-action programs include many of the following requirements:

1. Active recruiting of qualified candidates for jobs in which imbalances due to race or sex exist.
2. Not tolerating ethnic or sexual harassment or prejudice in the work environment.
3. Requiring all management personnel to conduct ongoing affirmative-action education programs for subordinates.
4. Setting goals and timetables to integrate women and minorities into management positions and nontraditional, nonmanagement positions. (Examples of nontraditional, nonmanagement jobs include: men in clerical jobs and women in outdoor labor jobs.)
5. Entering into contracts with suppliers and vendors whose companies are owned by minorities or women.
6. Designing facilities to make reasonable accommodations for handicapped individuals.

## Competitive Advantage Through People

In the last third of the twentieth century, effective human relations has become a key business strategy. The strategy centers on gaining a competitive advantage through people. This means an organization wins because of its people. To assure success, organizations have learned that they must promote a diverse work force, encourage healthy life-styles, and recognize that work and family issues overlap.

A diverse work force is a group of employees that includes men, women, and people of color with variations in age and physical ability. Businesses or organizations often try to maintain a diverse mix of employees. The value of this part of the human relations strategy is in its ability to meet diverse customer needs.

Healthy employees have good attendance records, positive attitudes, fewer injuries, and produce higher-quality products. For such reasons, organizations promote mental health and wellness programs. These programs may include help with exercise, advice on diet, and counseling for substance abuse. The Drug-Free Workplace Act of 1988 provides additional incentives for treatment and rehabilitation. The federal law allows for drug testing of employees.

Organizations have been slow to accept that work and family issues overlap. A strategy referred to as the *flexible workplace* is gaining widespread acceptance and use. The flexible workplace is an effort to help employees in the areas of:

- Parental leave for newborn children.
- Leaves of absence for elder care (aging or ailing parents).
- Advice and assistance with child care.
- Flexible reporting times for dealing with routine family illness.
- Half days or a few hours off to visit schools or to do charitable service work.

Other flexible workplace advantages often include opportunities for:

- Regular part-time work—working a regular schedule for less than 40 hours per week.

*Akos Szilvasi/Stock, Boston*

Illus. 1-7. Assistance with day care is a dimension of the flexible workplace.

- Telecommuting—working at home using a computer to communicate with others at work. *Tele* refers to the telephone or telephone lines.
- Secondary work locations—working at a different location other than your regular (primary) location.
- Phased retirements—working fewer and fewer hours during the last year of your job.

## SUCCESS THROUGH HUMAN RELATIONS

Success in any occupation requires knowledge and skills. Success just doesn't happen by chance. You have to make it happen. Everyone gets just about the same number of breaks in life. Those who are ready to take advantage of these breaks are the ones who succeed. Many people have opportunities to succeed but miss the chance because they are not ready. We never know exactly when opportunity will come, so we must be ready at all times. To be ready to succeed in your job, you must have two kinds of knowledge: technical knowledge and people knowledge.

### Technical Knowledge

*Technical knowledge* is what you know about the job itself. For example, a lawyer must know the law, a photographer must understand cameras, a cook must be familiar with the menu, and a bus driver must know the route and how to drive a bus. Technical knowledge is usually gained by taking classes.

*Photo by Richard Younker*

Illus. 1-8. A bus driver must have technical knowledge about the route and how to drive a bus.

Of course, there are other ways of gaining technical knowledge. For example, you may learn technical skills on the job. You may learn by making mistakes, and you may learn by observing others. The important thing is that, to begin any job, you must have some technical knowledge and skills.

## People Knowledge

To succeed in your job, you must have people knowledge. *People knowledge* means knowing how to get along with your co-workers and with your employer. People knowledge will help you serve customers better. People knowledge will even help you to understand yourself.

## Your Success Vehicle

Ideally, technical knowledge and people knowledge work together. When you combine the two, you have a vehicle for success. The *back wheels* of your success vehicle are your technical knowledge. These back wheels provide the power to get you where you want to go. The *front wheels* are your people knowledge. The direction you take in your career is determined by your knowledge. The particular direction you ought to move is upward. Yet some people move only horizontally, and others move up for a while and then stop or move downward. People knowledge enables you to find the proper roads to travel on your route to success.

People knowledge is human relations. Getting started in a job depends on technical knowledge, but success follows because of your knowledge of human relations. Regardless of your occupation, you must be able to work well with people.

In addition to job success, the increased use of human relations skills by you, your co-workers, and others in the employment environment will lead to a much higher quality of worklife. It is much more pleasant to work in an organization that runs smoothly and has little conflict or strife. When people are getting along with one another, a workplace has more production, fewer mistakes, lower employee turnover, and a general positive feeling of *esprit de corps* among people. Working to improve human relations at your place of employment is worthwhile for everyone concerned.

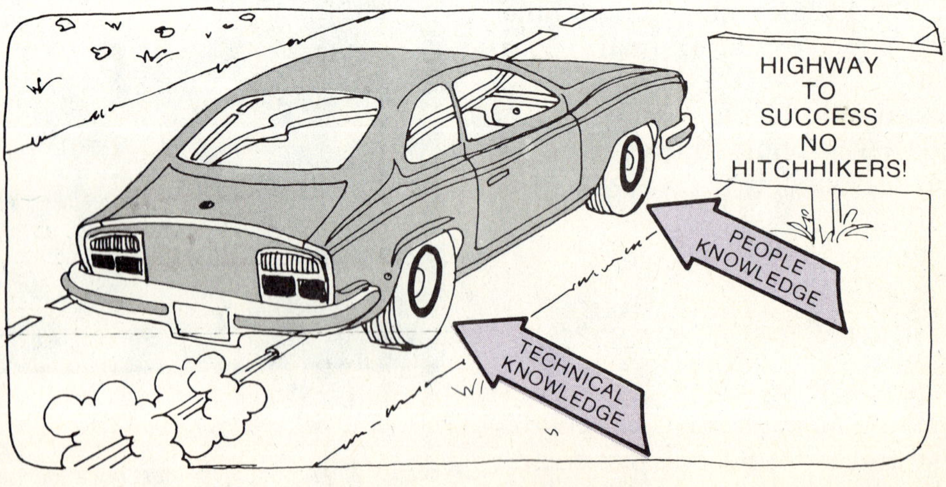


Illus. 1-9. Success vehicle.

# Activity 1-1

## Learning about Each Other

This activity will help you get to know the people in your class. You may already be acquainted with most or all of them. Nevertheless, by completing this activity, you may learn many things about them that you did not know before.

You need a partner for this activity. Choose someone you don't know very well. Get together with your partner so that the two of you can talk privately. Using the Interview Data Sheet as a guide, take turns interviewing each other. Write out the answer your partner gives to each question. If you do not understand the answer completely, ask your partner to keep talking and explain with more detail.

After you finish interviewing each other, introduce your partner to the class. Using the notes you wrote out during the interview, tell the class about your partner.

### Interview Data Sheet

Name of Interviewee ____________________

My Name ____________________

1. What year in school are you?

____________________

2. Do you work or give volunteer service? Describe some of the things you do.

____________________

____________________

3. What other schools have you attended?

____________________

____________________

____________________

4. Do you have any brothers or sisters? (If older brothers and/or sisters work, where do they work?) What is your birth order in your family?

____________________

____________________

____________________

5. Do you have any hobbies? What do you do in your spare time?

____________________

____________________

____________________

6. What is your "all-time" favorite movie? Favorite record?

____________________

____________________

____________________

7. What do you plan to do after graduation?

____________________

____________________

____________________

8. What is the most meaningful thing that happened to you in the past year?

____________________

____________________

____________________

# Activity 1-2

## Brainstorming Your Concerns

The purpose of this two-part activity is to identify some things you want to learn about human relations. After you complete this activity you will know more about the concerns of the members of your class. You will learn that others have different reasons for studying human relations.

### Part 1

You have five minutes to complete Part I of this activity. During this time period, write out a list of your problems or concerns about getting along with people. You may think of a few problems right away, but then you may not think of any problem for two or three minutes. During the last two minutes, you may think of some very important problems. It is important to use the *full five minutes!* Your teacher will tell you when to begin.

### Part 2

Your teacher will give you the next set of instructions for Part 2 of this activity. Use the spaces provided to classify the different concerns of the class. Write each concern or problem under the correct heading.

*People Knowledge—Self*

______________________________

______________________________

______________________________

______________________________

______________________________

______________________________

*People Knowledge—Co-Workers*

Example: Trying to get along with a co-worker who doesn't do his or her share of the work.

______________________________

______________________________

______________________________

______________________________

______________________________

______________________________

*People Knowledge—Employers*

______________________________

______________________________

______________________________

______________________________

______________________________

______________________________

*People Knowledge—Customers*

______________________________

______________________________

______________________________

______________________________

______________________________

______________________________

# Activity 1-3

## Human Relations with Other Students

During your study of human relations, you will be required to work closely with other students. To learn how to work successfully with other students, answer the following questions in the spaces provided.

1. How do you tell someone that you disagree with what he or she is saying?

2. What risks are involved in telling someone that you disagree?

3. How do you compliment someone when you like what he or she is saying?

4. Which is easier: to compliment a person or to disagree with a person? Explain your answer.

5. How can you ask a question when you're not sure of how to ask it?

6. What is the definition of a so-called dumb question?

7. When you do not understand something, what can you say besides, "I don't understand"?

8. List five qualities that describe your best friend. After you finish, your teacher will give further instructions.

______________________________

______________________________

______________________________

______________________________

______________________________

# Activity 1-4

## Self-Test

This activity is designed to measure your beginning understanding of human relations. To complete it, you should simply fill in the blanks with the correct word or group of words.

1. Understanding human relations can be both very simple and very ___________.

2. The term *human relations* refers to ___________ between people.

3. The different ___________ of people with which you will have relationships at work are ___________, ___________, and ___________.

4. Most businesses assume that the customer is always ___________.

5. The human relations movement began in the ___________.

6. The most significant experiment of the human relations movement took place in a ___________ factory.

7. It was the ___________ employees received during the experiment that caused their production to improve.

8. ___________ means that personnel activities are conducted without discrimination.

9. A positive movement toward a prejudice-free work environment is called ___________.

10. ___________ knowledge is what you know about the job itself.

11. ___________ knowledge is human relations.

12. Competitive advantage through people means an organization will ___________ because of its people.

13. The ___________ is an effort to help employees with child care, elder care, and time off for charitable service work.

Chapter 2

# Self-Esteem

KNOWLEDGE: After reading this chapter, you will be able to:

1. Describe self-esteem.
2. Define the term *self-image.*
3. Compare and contrast inner- and other-directed people.
4. Analyze strategies that enable people to gain self-knowledge.
5. Illustrate the valuing process and apply the process to values at work.
6. Define *justice* and discriminate between the three levels of practicing justice.
7. Describe a strategy for building self-confidence.
8. Identify characteristics of successful people.
9. Write short- and long-term goals.
10. Define the term *priorities.*
11. Describe the process of making trade-offs.

ATTITUDES: After reading this chapter, you will:

1. Want to develop a positive self-image.
2. Accept the ideals of the inner-directed person.
3. Value self-knowledge.
4. Judge issues and problems using higher-level concepts of justice.
5. Appreciate the value of being genuine, trusting, and confident.
6. Gain satisfaction from visualizing short- and long-term goals.
7. Be committed to setting personal priorities and be able to make rational trade-offs.

*Self-esteem* is the total of all you believe about yourself. It may be determined by your answers to the following questions.

- Who are you?
- What is important to you?
- Do you like yourself?
- Where are you going in life?

Our study of human relations begins with the most important relationship you have—the relationship you have with yourself.

## WHO ARE YOU?

How much do you know about yourself? Before you answer this question, try answering how you would describe yourself:

- to a friend?
- to a teacher?
- to your parents?
- to your supervisor at work?
- to yourself?

Do you realize that you might describe yourself differently depending upon the situation? Everybody does this; some do this more than others. Ideally you describe yourself in the same manner to everyone.

People describe themselves differently to different people for many reasons. The two main reasons are: (1) people have many selves, and (2) people try to put the best combination of their many selves forward.

### Rating Your Many Selves

You have many selves. For example, you may have:

- a friendly self.
- a romantic self.
- a greedy self.
- a modest self.
- an honest self.
- a clever self.
- a nosy self.
- an aggressive self.

Any one of these selves may be a part of a picture of you. Your own private defi-

Illus. 2-1. Your many selves.

nition of these selves is your *self-image.* In a way, your self-image is what you think of yourself. To get an idea of what you think of yourself, try rating yourself on the various scales shown in Illus. 2-2. Each scale ranges from 1 to 10. The highest rating is 10, the middle rating is 5, and the lowest rating is 1.

Each rating is a definition. The definition is what you mean by friendly, honest, greedy, and the like. The definition is personal. It is what you think of yourself. It is your self-image.

If you were to rate these different selves tomorrow, would the ratings change? The ratings might change because your moods do affect the way you feel about yourself. On the average, however, your ratings of yourself remain the same.

## Putting on Your Best Selves

Do you remember the second main reason people tend to describe themselves differently to different people? It centers on putting your best foot forward. When you are with someone, you try to put the best combination of your many selves forward. Understanding how you decide which selves to make known to others is important. By being aware of how such

**My Friendly Self**

| 10 | 9 | 8 | 7 | 6 | 5 | 4 | 3 | 2 | 1 |
|---|---|---|---|---|---|---|---|---|---|
| very friendly | | | | generally friendly | | | | | not friendly |

**My Honest Self**

| 10 | 9 | 8 | 7 | 6 | 5 | 4 | 3 | 2 | 1 |
|---|---|---|---|---|---|---|---|---|---|
| always honest | | | | usually honest | | | | | dishonest |

**My Greedy Self**

| 10 | 9 | 8 | 7 | 6 | 5 | 4 | 3 | 2 | 1 |
|---|---|---|---|---|---|---|---|---|---|
| not greedy | | | | somewhat greedy | | | | | very greedy |

**My Modest Self**

| 10 | 9 | 8 | 7 | 6 | 5 | 4 | 3 | 2 | 1 |
|---|---|---|---|---|---|---|---|---|---|
| always modest | | | | middle of the road | | | | | boastful |

Illus. 2-2. Self-image rating scale.

Illus. 2-3. Rating your self-image.

Illus. 2-4. Does the job applicant represent an inner-directed or other-directed person?

decisions are made, you can help yourself answer the question, Who are you?

People decide which of their many selves to reveal to others in four different methods. These are: (1) by doing what others expect, (2) by doing what others prescribe, (3) by acting on trial and error, and (4) by acting on personal beliefs. Each of these methods will be illustrated in this chapter. The use of each method will tell whether a person's behavior is other-directed, other- and inner-directed, or inner-directed.

### *Method 1: Doing What Others Expect*

When you talk with others, what you say and the way you act may be a result of what they expect from you. Bill is a person who does what others expect. He works after school and on weekends in a warehouse. His job is to load and unload trucks. The employees at the warehouse use rough language when they talk. Sometimes they grumble and swear about the poor working conditions in the warehouse. Bill joins in and swears with them because he believes they expect this from him.

At home Bill doesn't use foul language because he knows that his parents expect him not to swear. And when Bill is with his friends, he tends to brag slightly about his warehouse job because he thinks his friends expect him to be proud of his job. After all, he has the best-paying job among them.

Bill does what others expect him to do. People like Bill, who gear their behavior to what others expect, are *other-directed* people.

### *Method 2: Doing What Others Prescribe*

In Method 2 people decide, by prescription, which of their selves to put forward. Generally, a prescription is an order for medicine based upon a physician's diagnosis. The prescription is taken to a pharmacy, where medicine is obtained. When the medicine is taken by the person who is ill, that person usually gets better.

Taking someone's advice is like taking a prescription. You know that advice is coming when you hear people say:

- Why don't you . . .?
- If I were you, I'd. . . .
- If you were smart, you'd . . .?

Illus. 2-5. Doing what others expect.

- When are you going to . . .?
- Here is what you ought to do. . . .

People who depend upon others to tell, advise, and prescribe actions for them are also other-directed persons. Sally is an example of such a person. Sally constantly asks her co-workers what she should do. "Should I trade in my car? Should I go out with Jim? Should I change my typewriter ribbon? Should I go on a diet? Should I ask for a raise?" Sally finds security in asking others what to do. She is comfortable being a puppet whose actions are controlled by others.

People like Sally seek out prescriptions so that they don't have to think for themselves. To them, taking advice or prescriptions from others is safe. If another person's prescription does not work, it is not her fault. Sally and people like her fool themselves by thinking that the failure rests with the person giving the prescription. The person simply gave poor advice. The receiver of the prescription then looks for a *new* prescription. By following this procedure, advice-seekers need never *take responsibility for their own actions.*

### *Method 3: Acting by Trial and Error*

A person who uses the trial-and-error method in putting his or her best foot forward is continually experimenting. Carlos uses this method. When he isn't sure about something, he tries to figure out the situation. Then he gives himself a prescription. For example, Carlos believes that he is particularly good at figuring out his teachers. His class schedule reads like this:

- First period: No sweat, just talk a lot in class.
- Second period: Be cool, write a bunch on the test.
- Third period: OK, I'm on the team.
- Fourth period: Act tough, talk loud.
- Fifth period: Teacher's a pushover; she likes boy students more than girl students.

Illus. 2-6. Do you act as others prescribe?

Carlos uses what he knows about his teachers to make decisions. If something doesn't work, Carlos tries another tactic. If Carlos's next idea is unsuccessful, he tries something else. He tries to find out what others want or like. When he thinks he knows, he tries to get the other person to make life easy for him. Carlos watches the reactions of others very carefully. He must do this because his next move depends upon the reaction of others. People like Carlos are *other- and inner-directed* people.

### *Method 4: Acting on Personal Beliefs*

An *inner-directed* person decides which selves to put forward by acting on personal beliefs. These personal beliefs are logical and unemotional. The inner-directed individual asks the questions, With which of my selves am I most comfortable? With which of my selves am I most successful? This person then reveals the most logical combinations of these selves.

The actions of inner-directed people are based upon what they believe. They do not put up false fronts. They are not manipulated or used by others, and they themselves don't manipulate or use others. Because inner-directed people present the same set of selves to others most of the time, they are genuine. People who experience lasting success in their personal life or at work are inner-directed persons.

Stacy is an example of an inner-

Illus. 2-7. An inner-directed person acts on personal beliefs.

directed person. She knows which of her many selves she likes best. She also knows which is most successful. Stacy presents the same set of selves to her supervisor, her co-workers, her parents, and her friends.

For example, Stacy believes that getting a two-year degree from the local community college is important. She plans to enroll in this college next year. Although her parents do want her to go on to college, several of Stacy's friends and relatives have different opinions on the subject. Some of Stacy's friends see no future in going to college. Her supervisor at the store where she works graduated from a four-year college and thinks that a two-year degree won't be worth much. Stacy's grandparents don't want her to attend the local community college because many of their friends sent their children to private colleges. Finally two of Stacy's co-workers quit college after a year; they think that Stacy won't make it through college either. So, Stacy feels a lot of pressure on this subject.

To ease the pressures surrounding her, Stacy could use any one of the three methods already described. How do you think Stacy would use the following methods to adjust herself to this situation? Write your answers in the spaces provided.

Using Method 1 (doing what others expect), Stacy could tell her supervisor:

________________________________________

________________________________________

________________________________________

Tell her friends:

________________________________________

________________________________________

________________________________________

Using Method 2 (doing what others prescribe), Stacy could tell her co-workers:

________________________________________

________________________________________

________________________________________

Using Method 3 (acting by trial and error), Stacy could tell her grandparents:

________________________________________

________________________________________

________________________________________

But Stacy does not use any of these three methods of revealing her many selves. Stacy bases her actions on personal beliefs. She does not argue with people. She does not agree with people just to be agreeable. When asked her opinion of her plans, Stacy states what she believes. She makes the same statement to everyone. When others give opposite views, Stacy tries to understand why. Sometimes, of course, Stacy changes her views. Just because she has given her opinion about something does not mean that she cannot change her mind later on. However, when Stacy changes her mind, she does not try to hide it from certain people.

One must realize, however, that Method 4—acting on personal beliefs—is difficult to adopt. It's hard to continually be logical, unemotional, and confident that any decision made is sound.

The four methods of revealing yourself to others, and the results of these methods, are summarized in Table 2-1.

## Learning More about Yourself

How do you find out more about yourself? Generally there are two ways in which people learn about themselves over a lifetime: (1) by luck, and (2) by conscious effort.

### *Learning by Luck*

Learning about oneself by luck is characteristic of immature people. Such people go through their lives not knowing much about themselves. They wonder why they did something. They wonder why others react to them in certain ways. But they never try to find out. When these people do learn something about themselves, it is just through plain luck.

### *Learning by Conscious Effort: The Johari Window*

Increasing your self-knowledge requires some effort. To begin this effort, you must give and receive information about yourself. This giving and receiving process is shown in Illus. 2-8. The illustration is called the Johari Window because it was developed by Joseph Luft and Harry Ingham.

The Johari Window is like a picture of your personality. It represents four sections: (1) the arena, (2) the hidden section, (3) the blind spot, and (4) the unknown section.

***The Arena.*** The arena section of your Johari Window represents *information about you that you know and most of your friends know.* Notice the headings "Things I Know" and "Things Others Know" for the upper left block in Illus. 2-8.

Below are two examples of information about you which, if true, would be known to you and to most of your friends. Try to add two more examples.

| | Things I Know |
|---|---|
| *Things Others Know* | 1. I work at a TV station.<br>2. I have two brothers.<br>3. ____________<br>4. ____________ |

***The Hidden Section.*** The hidden section of your Johari Window contains *information about you that you know, but no one else knows.* This information is private. However, if someone asks you, you might give it.

Here are two examples of private or hidden things. Try to add two more.

| | Things I Know |
|---|---|
| *Things Others Don't Know* | *1. I want to own my own business.*<br>2. I enjoy being with my family.<br>3. ____________<br>4. ____________ |

| Action Based on | Person Described As | Result of Action |
|---|---|---|
| What others expect | Other-directed | Chameleon effect |
| What others prescribe | Other-directed | Puppet effect |
| Trial and error | Other- and inner-directed | Manipulation effect |
| Personal beliefs | Inner-directed | Genuine effect |

Table 2-1. Summary of other- and inner-directed behavior.

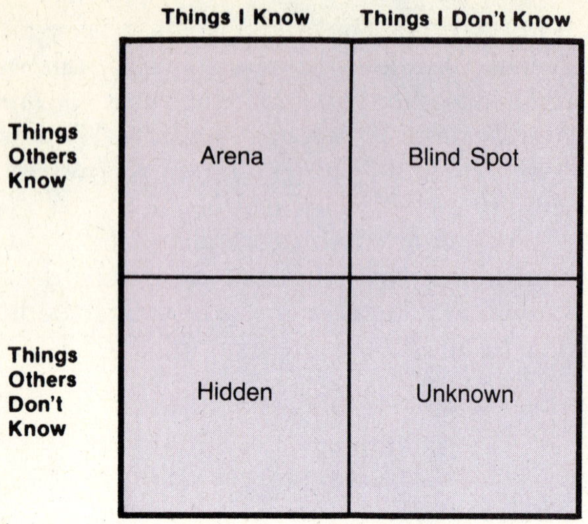


Illus. 2-8. The Johari Window.

***The Blind Spot.*** The blind spot of your Johari Window contains *information about you that you do not know,* and the interesting aspect of this section is that *others know this information about you.* For example, you may cough before you speak or you may curl your hair with a finger while you talk. The point is, others know this but you are not aware of doing it.

***The Unknown Section.*** The unknown section of your Johari Window represents the unconscious. This means that *neither you nor anyone knows about the information on you* in this section. For example, this section may contain memories from your early childhood. It also represents unexplored abilities. For example, some day you could be a great salesperson, but for now you have no idea that the ability to be a great salesperson is in you.

## Using Your Self-Knowledge

When you know yourself, you have a Johari Window that looks like Illus. 2-9.

Notice that the arena in Illus. 2-9 is the largest section of the window. This means that you give and receive information about yourself freely. Other people see you as honest and trustworthy because most of your behavior is open and straightforward. People do not have to guess about your intentions.

When your Johari Window has a large arena, this also means that you have much self-knowledge. The more self-knowledge you have, the better you understand who you are. And when you understand yourself, you can understand others better.

Understanding other people is essential to good human relations. Whenever you judge someone, you use yourself as the point of reference. For example, Mrs. Summers, a restaurant manager, asked Lisa, the assistant manager, about Tim's ability to serve customers. "Is Tim fast at taking food orders at the counter windows?"

When Lisa commented about Tim,

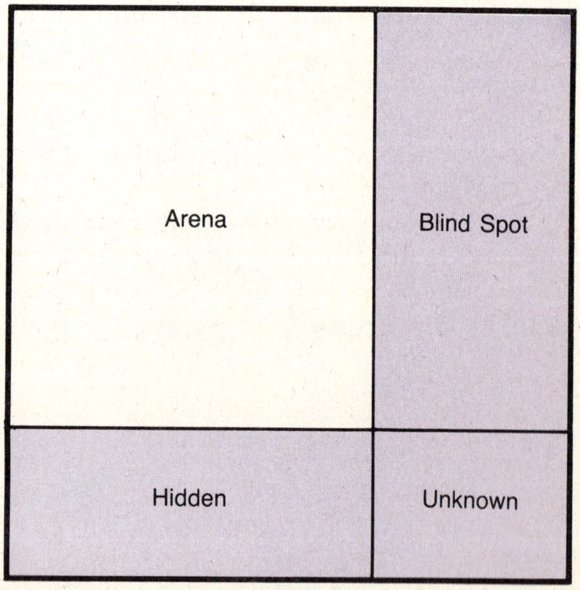


Illus. 2-9. The Johari Window of a person with much self-knowledge.

she used herself as the measuring device. She thought to herself: "Tim is about as fast as I am. Joe is much slower than I. And Tim is definitely faster then Joe." So she said, "Why, yes, Mrs. Summers, Tim is pretty good at window service."

Understanding yourself is especially important when personal feelings are involved. Suppose Mrs. Summers asked Joe, rather than Lisa, the same question. Joe may be jealous of Tim, so his answer may be affected by his feelings. However, if Joe has some self-understanding, he may think to himself: "Yes, Tim is pretty fast. He is so fast that he makes me look slow. It's kind of embarrassing. I could say he's just OK at the windows. Or I could say he's fast because we do all the cleaning up for him while he takes orders from customers. That's partly true. Oh, what the heck, I might as well admit it. Tim is pretty good at the order windows."

Joe is aware of his negative feelings for Tim. Joe also knows why, but he doesn't try to hide it from himself with excuses. Joe understands himself. Which of the two Johari Windows in Illus. 2-10 do you think belongs to Joe?

If you answered B, you are correct. Window B has the larger arena. At the end of this chapter, you will find a questionnaire that will enable you to plot your own Johari Window. By filling out the questionnaire, you can measure your self-knowledge and then use it to understand yourself and others better.

## Brain Dominance Theory

Learning by conscious effort also includes being aware of your behavior traits. For example:

- ▶ Do you like to be on time, and are you upset if others are not on time?
- ▶ Do you like to initiate conversation, or do you let others start a discussion?
- ▶ Are you good at planning, but not so good at following through with the details of the plans?

The answers to these questions may be related to your brain orientation.

### *The Discovery of Two Sides of the Brain*

The study of brain orientation is often referred to as *brain dominance theory.*

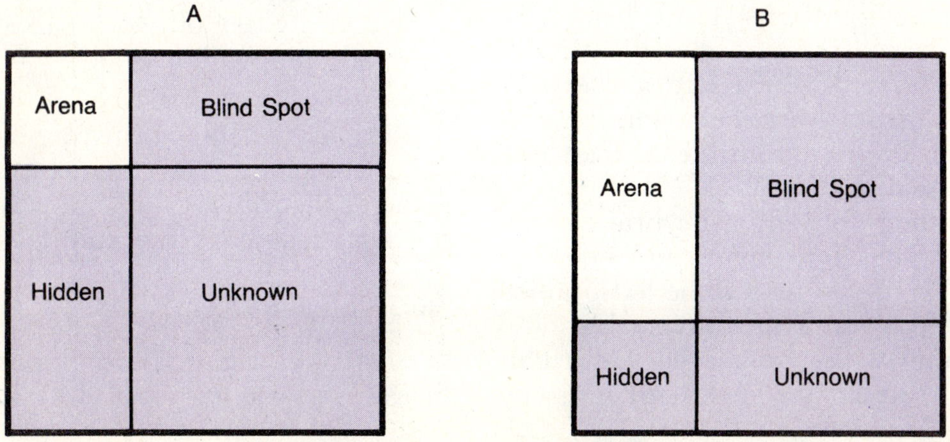


Illus. 2-10. Which is Joe's Johari Window?

Brain dominance means that the way you think and behave depends on which side (or hemisphere) of your brain is the more influential. This theory is based on the fact that the human brain has two sides, and each side operates independently. The discovery of "independent sides" was made by Dr. Roger Sperry in the early 1960s. For his work, Dr. Sperry received a Nobel Prize in 1981.

Other scientists and doctors used Sperry's discovery in their own work. Many of these scientists began studies to find out which side of the brain performed certain tasks. They found that the *left* side of the brain controls the *right* side of the body, while the *right* side of the brain controls the *left* side of the body.

### *Left- and Right-Brain Behavior*

The *left* side of the brain controls the speaking ability for most people. The *right* side of the brain controls humor and emotion. Yet, not all researchers agree on which behaviors are controlled by the left or the right side of the brain.[1]

Before reading further, complete Activity 2-9 on page 73. That Activity may give you some idea of your brain orientation and associated behaviors.

Behavior patterns have been discovered from scientific classification of tasks performed by the left or the right side of the brain. These behaviors, and the side of the brain responsible for them, are summarized in Illus. 2-11.

Use the information on brain dominance to help you understand behavior tendencies. If you tend to be left-brained yourself, you may be uncomfortable in relationships with those who are right-brained. Similarly, those with a strong right-brain orientation may be uncomfortable with those who are left-brained. Knowing this, you can learn to value people with strengths that are the opposite of yours. Many effective work teams have members with left- and right-brained dominance. Each member then makes up for the deficiencies in other members. The result is a well-balanced team.

It is important to note that neither a left- nor a right-brain orientation is better than the other. The most desirable orientation is one that is balanced. This is referred to as *whole-brain thinking.*

## WHAT IS IMPORTANT TO YOU?

Everyone has values. *Values* are personal beliefs that tell you what is desirable and worthwhile. Values also tell you what is right or just. Your values help you decide what is important and help you determine what choices to make in your everyday life. When you are at work, you must make value judgments.

To get a better idea of what values are, complete the following sentences:

- I'm for. . . .
- I'm against. . . .
- On Friday night I usually. . . .
- On my day off work I like to. . . .
- I enjoy reading about. . . .

The statements you wrote say something about you. The statements indicate some of the things you believe are or are not worthwhile or desirable.

### The Value System

Just as everyone has lungs and a heart, everyone has a personal value sys-

1. Ann Gibbons, "New Maps of the Human Brain," *Science* (July 13, 1990), pp. 122–123.

Illus. 2-11. Behaviors associated with the left or right hemispheres of the brain.

tem. The value system works by processing thoughts and ideas. Some thoughts and ideas are used, while others are thrown away. Those thoughts and ideas that are used by a person become his or her values. All value systems work the same way, but the thoughts and ideas that become values are different from one person to another.

## *How People's Values Are Different*

To show you how values differ, try to answer this question: How much money is a lot of money? Write your answer in the space below.

Answer: $________

Now compare your answer with the answers of your classmates. Are there many different answers? There are probably as many answers as there are students in the class.

Try one more question: How many people live in a small town? Just to make it a little more difficult for you, try to guess what others will say.

Your answer:

_____ people live in a small town.

Your guess of what others will say:

_____ people live in a small town.

Again compare your answers with those of your classmates. Look for two things. First, how many people had the same answer? (Probably not very many.) Second, were you lucky enough to guess what someone's answer was?

There are two points to this guessing game. First, almost everyone has a different answer. This is because people have different values. Second, with some luck you may guess what one or two people wrote about the size of small towns. It is hard to guess what others value because people's values are different. You may agree with some. With others you may be close to agreement. Yet, with some people you may disagree completely.

## *Factors That Affect Values*

Values differ because of the many factors that affect the formation of values. Table 2-2 shows a list of these factors. Look at the list and ask yourself:

Illus. 2-12. How much money is a lot of money?

- ▶ Which people affect my values?
- ▶ Which places affect my values?
- ▶ Which things affect my values?

## *How the Value System Works*

Illus. 2-13 is a diagram that shows how the value system works. Look at this diagram and note that the starting point of the value system is an idea. All ideas are connected to one or more of three sources. The three sources are: people, places, and things.

*People* includes parents, relatives, friends, neighbors, teachers, employers, and co-workers. *Places* include the part of the country in which you live or have lived in the past. Places also include the size of the town or city in which you live (or have lived). The type and size of the school you attend (or have attended) are also a part of places. *Things* means radio and TV programs, movies, books, tapes, compact disks (CDs), video cassettes, newspapers, magazines, computer games and software, and so on. All of these items are sources of ideas for you.

| People | Places | Things |
|---|---|---|
| Parents | Countries in which you have lived | Radio |
| Friends | Part of the country you live (have lived) in—North, South, East, West | TV, VCR |
| Employer(s) | Part of town where you live | Movies |
| Co-workers | Schools you attend | Books, magazines |
| Relatives | Places you visit | Newspapers |
| Neighbors | | Tapes, CDs |
| Teachers | | Computers |
| Members of the community | | |

Table 2-2. Factors that affect values.

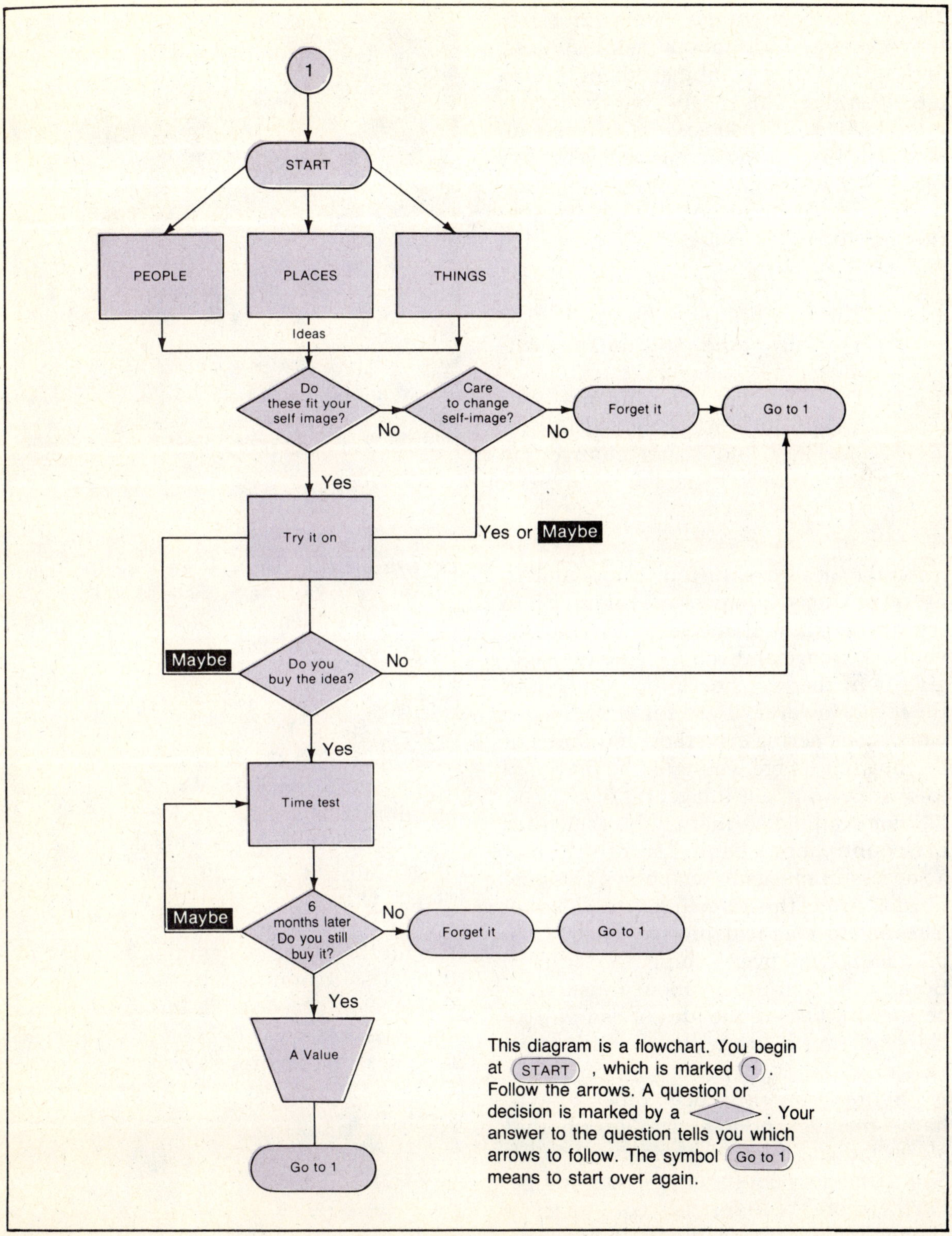


Illus. 2-13. How the value system works.

***Ideas and Self-Image.*** Your value system processes ideas (about people, places, and things) and combines them into a *possible* value. This means that the idea is *not* a value at this stage; it is still just an idea. The first question that comes to your mind is, *Does the idea fit my self-image?*

There are three possible answers to this question. These are:

1. The idea fits my self-image.
2. The idea does *not* fit my self-image.
3. The idea does *not* fit my self-image, but it might be worth considering; and I can change my self-image a little.

Illus. 2-14. William is listening to classical music.

If the idea fits with your personal definition of you, you may or may not wish to try on the idea. If the idea does not fit your self-image and you have no desire to give it further consideration, you forget the idea. However, if you think the idea is worth considering even though it does not fit your self-image, you must be prepared to change your self-image.

For example, William plays the guitar in a country music band. Recently, he met a successful musician who plays classical music. After this meeting, the idea of *listening* to classical music—Bach, Chopin, and Beethoven—came to William. Because his self-image about music is to be a *little* different, the idea of listening to classical music fits with William's self-image.

Suppose another idea comes to William—the idea of joining a group that *plays* classical music. This idea is too different and does not fit with his self-image. Furthermore, William does not choose to change his self-image about country music. Therefore, William forgets this idea.

***Trying on the Idea.*** If an idea fits your self-image, you may wish to try it on. Even if the idea does *not* fit your self-image, you may want to try it on if you don't mind changing your self-image. Trying on the idea is the next step in the value system. It means actually doing something with the idea.

Let us go back to William's idea of listening to classical music. Suppose he decides that this idea fits his definition of himself and he cares to change his self-image. This means that the idea is still alive and has a possible value. William tries on the idea by beginning to listen to some classical music.

Once you have tried on an idea, the next question is, *Do I accept the idea?* The three possible answers are:

1. Yes.
2. No.
3. Maybe.

If your answer is yes, you may wish to give this idea the time test. If your answer is no, the flowchart of the value system in Illus. 2-13 reads as follows: Try it on. In other words, keep trying the idea for awhile.

After listening to classical music for awhile, William makes a decision. If he does not buy the idea, he forgets it. If his answer is maybe, he decides to keep listening to classical music for a while longer. Then he asks the question again, Do I buy the idea? If William's answer is yes, the idea is ready for the time test.

***The Time Test.*** If an idea is to become a value, it must last. The time test is about six months. Anytime before six months pass, your value system may classify the idea as a fad. A *fad* is something a person does for a short time only. Some of the more famous fads in the United States were C.B. radios, pet rocks, Rubik cubes, hula hoops, and spiking hair like a "new wave" music star.

If after six months you are still unsure of the idea, your value system will continue the time test.

***Accepting the Idea as a Value.*** If you buy the idea a year after you first considered it, the idea becomes a value. This value is now a definite part of you. It permanently helps you decide not only what is desirable and worthwhile, but also what is right and just.

## Values Relating to Justice

All problems that require decisions about what is right relate to justice. What is right may also be called what is just. Every day people who work in businesses must make decisions about what is just. Values help people make judgments about what is right.

For example, everyone agrees that stealing is wrong. Suppose a man steals medicine to save his child's life. He steals the medicine because he does not have enough money to buy it from a pharmacist who refused to sell the medicine at a lower price. Should this man be put in jail for stealing to save his child's life? How would you decide the answer in this situation? This part of the chapter will help you understand values about justice and how to decide what is right in a given situation.

People make decisions about what is right by basing their decisions on one of three reasons: (1) concern for power, (2) concern for rules and orders, and (3) concern for human rights. Sometimes a person will use a combination of these three reasons, but the decision is always based on one or more of these reasons.

### *Concern for Power*

Concern for power has two parts: physical power and nonphysical power. The latter is also referred to as *clout.*

The use of physical power means "might makes right." A person using physical power to decide what is right says, "You either do what I believe is right or you will be punished." The neighborhood bully often behaves this way. Wars are fought and terrorists try to impose their will on others because of the belief that physical power will decide who is right.

Take the example of Scott and his younger brother, Ed. Both of them worked at a convenience food store. Scott saw Ed take $10 from the cash register and put it in his pocket. During their morning break, Scott told Ed that he saw him take the money and warned him to put it back or else he would beat up Ed. Ed knew that Scott would beat him up, so Ed decided to put the money back in the cash register. But just before Ed put the

Illus. 2-15. Ed's concern for Scott's physical power makes him decide to return the money.

money back, he offered to split it with Scott—$5 each. Scott refused and just shook his fist at Ed.

The second part of concern for power is nonphysical. In this case, justice is defined as "You scratch my back and I'll scratch yours." This means that, if you do me a favor, I will pay you back with a favor. Whether you like the person or not is unimportant.

Doing favors also includes the use of clout. *Clout* generally means that, because of past favors or favoritism that you have shown, you can "pull strings" to get something done or have it your way.

### *Concern for Rules and Orders*

When people practice justice because of their concern for rules and orders, they do so because they respect rules and the authority who makes these rules. People who use this reason believe that it is their duty to follow rules or orders *without exception*. This reason also encourages people to do the right thing only because it pleases others.

For example, Mary was driving her sister Alice home one night after work. Mary had her lights on the high beam so that she could see down the road. As a car approached from the opposite direction, Mary did not switch her lights to the low beam. Alice asked Mary why she didn't switch the lights. Mary said she didn't think of it. Alice then told Mary that it was courteous and polite to switch to a low beam so that the other drivers could see better. In this situation, Alice was trying to persuade Mary to do the right thing because "nice people do behave this way."

A short time later, another car passed and again Mary did not dim her lights. This time Alice told Mary that the state's driving laws required her to dim her lights whenever a car passed in the opposite direction. In this situation, Alice was trying to persuade Mary to dim her lights based on the need to follow rules and orders.

Illus. 2-16. Alice is persuading Mary to follow rules and orders.

## *Concern for Human Rights*

The concern for human rights is a reason that is based on both written and unwritten laws. The Bill of Rights in the Constitution of the United States is an example of written laws that support this reason. Here justice means what is right for everyone in the world. When a person bases a decision on concern for human rights, he or she places respect for individuals as people *above* blind obedience to authority and to written rules.

For example, Tod is a high school student who works part time. He needed a good used car to drive to work and school. So he went to a used car lot. He explained to the salesperson just what he needed and how much he could afford to pay each month. After looking at several models, Tod narrowed his decision to two cars. Both were of similar quality, but one cost $700 more than the other. The more expensive car was a little more attractive in style. Tod would have preferred this car, but he knew he would have very little money left because of the higher monthly payment.

Now Roger, the salesperson, knew that he could use the bigger commission on selling the higher-priced car to pay his bills. Besides, Roger had orders from the car lot owner to sell as many higher-priced cars as possible. Furthermore, Roger knew that he could talk Tod into buying the more expensive car.

However, Roger believed that Tod's needs would be served very well by the lower-priced car. This way Tod would have some money left from his paycheck for other things. Roger also believed that, even though it would be in the best interest of the car lot owner and himself to sell the more expensive car, it would be morally wrong to sell an unnecessarily higher-priced car to Tod. So Roger decided to sell Tod the lower-priced car.

When you make decisions about what is right, try to use concern for human rights to help you make these decisions. By doing this you will improve your relations with the people involved in these decisions.

### Managing by Values

Effective managers of businesses or organizations manage by values. This means that such managers know:

1. What is important to themselves and to those who work with them.
2. What is good for the business or the organization.
3. How to decide what is right based on a concern for human rights.
4. How to apply this knowledge to their day-to-day actions.

Here are some value statements that some managers use to guide their decision making:

- Conduct business affairs with integrity.
- Confront and constructively resolve any incident of disrespect.
- Encourage innovation and creativity when solving problems.
- Be a profitable growth company.
- Treat all employees as individuals without regard to race, gender, or physical disability.

For managers, as for anyone, choosing or deciding is much easier when values are clear. If you are a manager or intend to be one, consider practicing "Superman" or "Superwoman" management. These comic book characters believed in "truth, justice, and the American way." These were their values. At work, "Superman" or "Superwoman" management means:

1. We never lie to ourselves or to our customers.
2. We treat one another and our customers fairly.
3. We provide a product or a service at a competitive price.

## DO YOU LIKE YOURSELF?

Liking yourself may be one of the most important things you'll have to do before you can achieve success. When you like yourself, you have self-confidence. And when you have self-confidence, your chances for success in the things you want to do are great. Liking yourself does not mean that you feel superior to others. Liking yourself means you have a positive self-image.

### Success and Your Self-Image

When you have a *positive self-image,* it means that you feel confident about your abilities and feelings. On the other hand, when you have a *negative self-image,* it means that you don't think much of yourself. Having a positive self-image can be the difference between success and failure. According to a famous doctor who made a detailed study of the self-image, you act like the person you conceive yourself to be.

Let us take a look at some examples. Al believed that he was dumb in math. Sure enough, his report card usually had very low grades in math. Joyce believed that she was quiet and shy. Because she felt this way, she rarely had a date. Linda believed that she was a good mechanic. As a result of this belief, Linda could repair her own car. Pedro believed that he had leadership abilities. He ran for office in his club and served as a group leader in his church.

From the above examples, you can conclude that both Al and Joyce have negative self-images that prevent them from being successful. Although Al may never get A's in math, he could do much better with a positive self-image. Joyce may never win a public speaking contest,

Illus. 2-17. Linda's success as a mechanic leads to a positive self-image.

but with a positive self-image she could have more dates.

You can also conclude that Linda and Pedro have positive self-images because they are experiencing some success. Of course, Linda may not know how to fix her car every time something goes wrong with it, but her positive self-image will allow her to be successful most of the time. Pedro may lose some elections in the future, but his positive self-image will enable him to keep trying.

## How to Attain a Positive Self-Image

Here are six specific things you can do to attain a positive self-image: (1) accept yourself, (2) recognize your strengths and weaknesses, (3) overcome your fears, (4) engage in positive self-talk, (5) maintain good physical health, and (6) manage stress.

### *Accept Yourself*

If you want to have a positive self-image, you start by accepting yourself just as you are, here and now. If you want to become a better person, accept yourself first. Then you can change.

Some people never accept themselves and are constantly trying to change their personalities. They overlook the importance of self-acceptance. Trying to change without first accepting yourself is like trying to climb out of quicksand. The harder you try, the more impossible it becomes.

### *Recognize Your Strengths and Weaknesses*

Self-accepting individuals know their strong points and weak points. Strong points are called personal strengths, and weak points are called personal weaknesses. Everyone has both personal strengths and weaknesses.

In the space below, write a few of your personal strengths and weaknesses.

Personal Strengths

______________________________

______________________________

______________________________

Personal Weaknesses

______________________________

______________________________

______________________________

If you are like most people, your list of weaknesses is longer than your list of strengths. Your list of weaknesses was also probably easier to write. Most people can recognize their weaknesses much more easily than they can recognize their strengths.

***What to Do with Weaknesses.*** Self-accepting people recognize their weaknesses but do not dwell upon them. Successful people maintain their composure in spite of their weaknesses. This means that they do not "go to pieces" over a mistake.

For example, in a game situation a player who makes a mistake and worries about it tends to make more mistakes. Being 100 percent ready for the next play means full concentration. Worrying about a mistake on a previous play hurts concentration. A player cannot be fully ready for the next play by dwelling on previous mistakes. Coaches want players who can shake off mistakes and keep going.

*Frank Siteman/Stock, Boston*

Illus. 2-18. A good player must be able to shake off mistakes and concentrate on the next play.

***What to Do with Strengths.*** Successful people know their strong points and take advantage of them. This means that they put their personal strengths to work for themselves. They do not let their weaknesses hurt them.

For example, let us look at Herb, the assistant night manager of the Lucky Strike Bowling Alley. Herb is quite proud of his job because he worked hard to get it. Before he was promoted to his present position, Herb did just about every kind of job at Lucky Strike. It did not take him long to learn that he was *not* good at working with the automatic pinsetters (a weak point). But he enjoyed working at the desk and dealing with customers (a strong point).

One day the manager told Herb to fix the pinsetter on lane 12. Herb dreaded this task because he could not fix mechanical things easily. So, Herb said, "I can do it, but Sandy can fix it in about half the time it will take me to do it." This was hard for Herb to say, but he knew that he could show his worth to the manager in other ways. Because Herb could not fix mechanical things easily did not mean he was a failure at Lucky Strike. Herb knew that he could do the work at the front desk better than any of his co-workers. So he excelled at what he could do well. He did not let his weaknesses hurt him in his overall performance on the job.

## *Overcome Your Fears*

No one is born confident. And no one is born with fear. Both being confident and being afraid are characteristics that are learned. The list of fears people have is endless. Here are some examples of fears that keep people from being successful.

- Fear of what others think or say.
- Fear of losing a job.

- ▶ Fear of failure in school.
- ▶ Fear of physical pain.
- ▶ Fear of competition.
- ▶ Fear of investing time and money.

The truth is that 99 percent of all things people fear or worry about never happen. If you could redirect all the energy wasted on worrying into ways of taking advantage of strong points, you could be successful beyond all dreams. Yet, the problem is there: People do have fears. And to dismiss these fears with the old saying that "it's all in your imagination" doesn't work. Fear is fear, whether it is real or imagined. This powerful force destroys confidence and makes people mental cripples.[2]

***Recognize That Fear Exists.*** In learning to be more confident, the first step is to recognize that fear exists. You must know what your fear is before you can do anything to overcome it.

***Take Action to Eliminate Fear.*** When you know what your fear is and you do nothing about it, the fear grows and grows. Taking action to eliminate fear means more than simply "hoping for the best." It means actually doing something.

A good example of people experiencing fear frequently occurs in social relationships. At this very moment, someone is planning to ask another person to go on a date. We can increase the fear factor by about 100 if the person asking has never asked this particular person out. When you finally take action by speaking with the person, fear vanishes.

The case of Sara is a different example. Sara is a salesperson who goes from door to door selling cosmetics. For the last two months, sales have been down. Yesterday her supervisor called her in the office for the third time this month. Her supervisor laid it on the line and said, "Get those sales up or you may lose your job." Sara is worried about her appearance, her sales presentation, her bookkeeping, and the possibility of losing her job. She recognizes all these fears, but her action is limited because she is only "hoping for the best." What action should Sara take?

Illus. 2-19. Sara the worrywart.

When people feel tense or anxious, they usually act in one of several ways. In Sara's case, she might get rid of her fears by talking to her supervisor, finding a job other than sales, or "making do" with her situation. Failure to take action will probably result in stress. The ways to reduce stress are presented on page 43.

## *Engage in Positive Self-Talk*

Everyone talks to himself or herself. On any particular day we probably talk to ourselves as much or more than we talk to other people. Certainly we don't talk out

2. For a more detailed examination of overcoming fear, see David J. Schwartz, *The Magic of Thinking Big* (Englewood Cliffs, NJ: Prentice-Hall, 1990). Parts of this section are inspired by the writings of Dr. Schwartz.

loud or vibrate our vocal chords, yet we do have self-conversations.

Our awareness of this self-talk is heightened when we criticize ourselves, and most of us are very good at self-criticism. Positive self-talk is a way to stop the criticism. Generally we don't like to be around people who are negative and criticize a lot. When we are negative with ourselves, it hurts our self-image.

To avoid or minimize self-criticism, we can change negative self-talk to positive self-talk. Here are six starters:

Negative Self-Talk

- I shouldn't have done. . . .
- Why did I do . . .?
- I can't. . . .
- I hate. . . .
- I really messed up. . . .
- Why do people make me feel . . .?

Positive Self-Talk

- Next time I will. . . .
- It's not like me to do that.
- Maybe I can't, but this is what I can do. . . .
- That's not always true.
- OK, so what? What's the worst possible thing that can happen?
- Nobody makes me feel a certain way. I choose how I feel, and I choose to feel good.

Positive self-talk can help you change your attitude toward a person, a project, or a problem. Use positive self-talk to change any negative or stressful situation. If you talk to yourself according to the suggestions given above, you can resolve difficult situations now. Why carry things around with you that hurt your self-image?

### *Maintain Good Physical Health*

Good physical health is important to a good self-image. It is not easy to like ourselves if we are overweight or underweight, or poisoning our bodies with tobacco, alcohol, or other drugs.

The remarkable thing about good physical health is that it is so visible. The old saying about "bright eyes and a bushy tail" still rings true. People who have good physical health look good, have lots of energy, and are fun to be with.

Many businesses and organizations recognize the importance of good physical health. Employees are encouraged to exercise and eat properly. To demonstrate the value of healthy employees, some companies:

1. Provide exercise facilities for workouts before work, during the lunch period, and after work.
2. Participate in corporate track events at the local, regional, or national levels.

Illus. 2-20. Being physically fit is important to a good self-image.

3. Sponsor road-running events for charity.
4. Offer diet counseling.
5. Restrict smoking to specific areas in buildings.

In addition, company health insurance plans will generally treat alcohol and drug addiction as a medical problem. This means that individual counseling and rehabilitation costs are covered by insurance in much the same way as illness and surgery expenses. The value of good health is clearly recognized in such business practices.

### *Manage Stress*

Exercise and diet are two good ways to maintain your health. But regular physical activity and proper eating habits won't guarantee a clean bill of health. Some jogging enthusiasts and health-food fans have more than their share of illnesses. What causes illness is the manner in which people approach their activities and eating habits.

Doctors who study chronic illnesses believe that as many as 70 percent of these illnesses are stress-related. This means that such things as sleeping problems, peptic ulcers, and even migraine headaches are related to stress. Indigestion is another way our bodies respond to the everyday stresses of life. Stomachaches are often a physical symptom of prolonged or excessive stress.

If you think about this, it makes a lot of sense. Derek's sleeping problems are a good example. Derek always has trouble falling asleep the night before an exam. His sleeping problem is an indication of his concern about doing well on the exam. His inability to sleep shows that emotions and the everyday stresses of his life do influence what happens to his health.

Stress symptoms also occur at work. Joan's anxiety over her performance appraisals is a good example. After she received a low rating and was passed over for a promotion, Joan began to lose effectiveness in her job. She complained of being tired all the time, and the sparkle in her eye was gone. Joan's reaction to her performance appraisal demonstrates the mental impact of stress.

Both Derek and Joan can learn to manage the stresses in their lives. An effective way to overcome stress is to avoid stress-producing situations. But it is not always possible to avoid situations that provoke stress. Derek can't avoid exams if he plans to graduate. And Joan can't avoid performance appraisals if she wants to stay in her job. What Derek and Joan can do is to use stress in a positive way. Instead of merely coping with stress, they can actively manage what happens in their everyday lives. Both of them have the power to overcome stress by taking charge of those things that can be changed.

For example, if Derek has a habit of cramming the night before exams, he can start a regular study program. If Joan can never find her weekly reports, she can put an end to her anxiety by cleaning up her work area. Such tensions can be managed positively. The important thing to remember is that stress can be a positive thing when it energizes you instead of slowing you down. If you learn to avoid stressful situations or manage those that can't be avoided, you will have more energy for creative projects and recreational activities.

## DO OTHERS LIKE YOU?

If people like you, it is because you possess certain qualities that make you likable. Some important qualities are given below. Try to add to this list of qualities in the spaces provided.

1. Being a good sport.
2. Being easy to talk with.
3. Having a good sense of humor.
4. Dressing nicely.
5.
6.
7.
8.
9.
10.

While there are many other valuable qualities that make a person likable, the two qualities that make people like a person *best* are: (1) being genuine, and (2) being trustworthy.

## Be a Genuine Person

Being genuine means being yourself. Genuine people do not put up false fronts to try to look good. Genuine people do not put on an act. Genuine people are comfortable with themselves.

The value of being genuine can be illustrated by looking at what makes a successful life insurance salesperson. In order to succeed in selling life insurance, the salesperson must possess many important qualities. But, first of all, the salesperson must be genuine because this particular job usually requires *more than one contact* with a prospective customer. If the prospective customer does not see this salesperson as a genuine human being during the first meeting, chances are that the salesperson will not succeed in making a sale.

Several studies have already been made by executives in the insurance business which indicate that most people buy insurance *because they like the salesperson.* The name of the insurance company represented by the salesperson is usually *not* the main reason why people buy insurance.

One large insurance company wanted to increase its sales. It conducted an expensive and time-consuming study to find out if sales might be related to the type of salesperson. The executives of this company wondered, for example, if the pushy, hard-sell type is more successful than the soft-sell type. Or does the good-looking, outgoing person produce more sales than the average-looking, quiet person? To find the answers to these questions, a test was given to all the top insurance salespersons of this company. The results of this study showed that:

1. The fast-talking, hard-hitting person sells no more insurance than the slow-talking, easygoing person.
2. The average-looking person sells just as much insurance as the good-looking person.

In other words, *no particular type of salesperson sold more insurance than other types of salespersons.* The study concluded that only one single factor is related to sales: *genuineness.* The most effective salespersons of this company were genuine because they reflected their *own* personalities and knew how to use their *own* abilities. These particular salespersons did not try to be like someone else.

The horizontal line in Illus. 2-20 and the vertical line in Illus. 2-21 show parts of the test that were given to the insurance salespersons. Both lines are divided into four equal parts. Read the brief descriptions given in these illustrations.

Now try this test by putting an X in one of the four sections of the horizontal

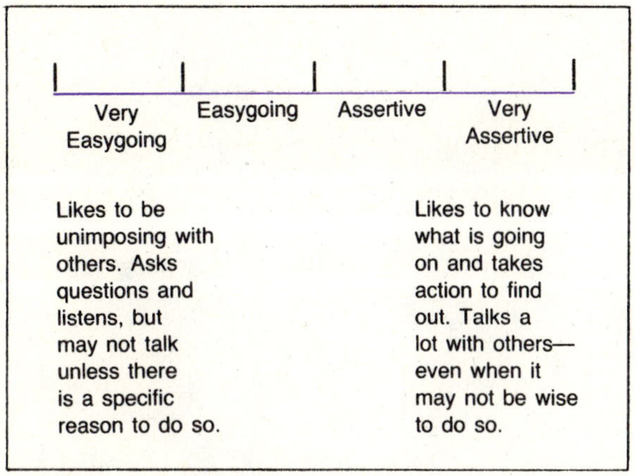


Illus. 2-21. Horizontal line showing degree of assertiveness.

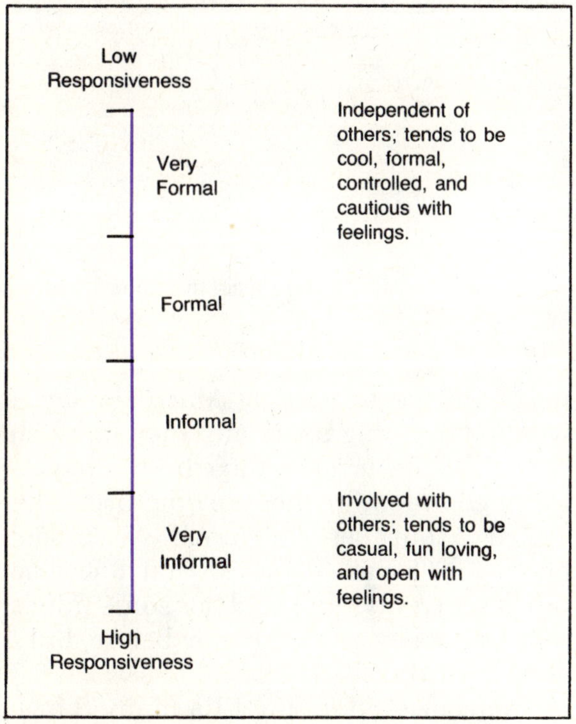


Illus. 2-22. Vertical line showing degree of responsiveness.

line and the vertical line. For example, if you believe that you are very assertive, place an X in the farthest section to the right of the horizontal line in Illus. 2-21. And if you believe that you are very informal, place an X in the lowest section of the vertical line in Illus. 2-22.

Illus. 2-23 shows how Laura plotted her X's on the horizontal line and the vertical line. Her X's have been transferred to the personality grid in Illus. 2-24. After you have plotted your X's on the lines in Illus. 2-21 and 2-22, transfer them to the grid in Illus. 2-24. Remember that the insurance company study showed that each type of person sells about the same amount of insurance. This means that each of the styles on the grid can be successful.

## Be a Trustworthy Person

When you are trustworthy, it means that others take risks with you because they have confidence in your abilities. The two key terms to understand here are *risk* and *confidence.*

Taking a risk means taking a chance. The greater the risk of anything, the more trust is involved. For example, how often do you count your change when you buy something.? Well, it probably depends on the amount of change you should receive. Say you buy a soft drink and pay for it with a one-dollar bill. Since your change will be small, you probably do not count it very closely. But suppose you pay for the soft drink with a ten-dollar bill. Chances are that you will count your change more carefully than you would when only one dollar is involved. You do this because your risk of loss is greater when ten dollars is involved.

The other part of being trustworthy is related to confidence. Assume for a moment that you are at a basketball game. The score is tied 60 to 60, and only five seconds remain to end the game. The team you are rooting for gets the ball and quickly calls "time out." Which player will the coach pick to take the last shot?

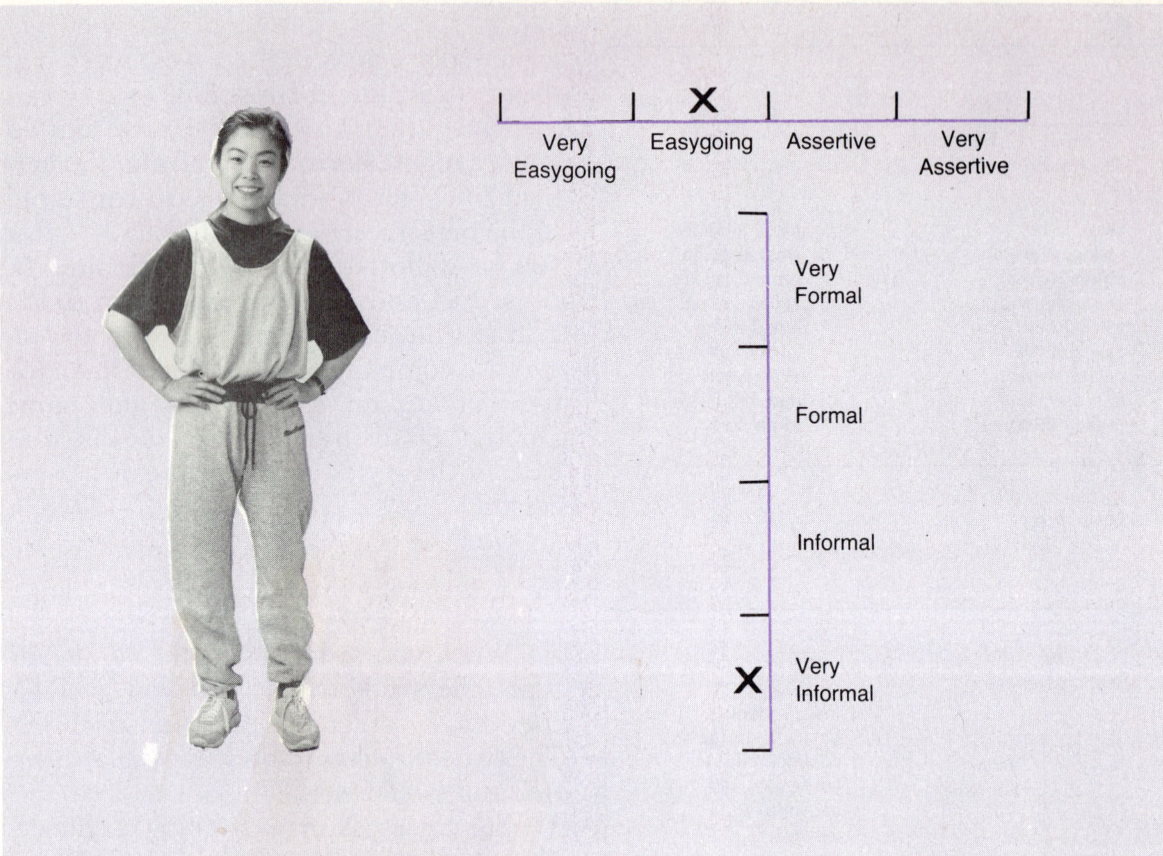


Illus. 2-23. Laura thinks of herself as easygoing and very informal. Her X's on the profile are shown above.

Naturally the coach will choose the best player. The coach chooses this player because the coach has confidence in this player's ability to get the job done.

## How to Build Trusting Relationships

The key to building trusting relationships with others is to be trustworthy yourself. When others take risks with you, you must prove that their risks are worth taking. And when others show confidence in you, you must justify their confidence by being reliable.

One way to establish a trusting relationship with someone is to risk being open about yourself. Consider the case of Maria, who met Ella for the first time. This is what Maria had to say:

"I started to work at Macy's today. I went on morning break and then to lunch with Ella. She is not my age but we have a lot in common. At the morning break we talked about her. At lunch we talked about me. I was surprised that I said so much about myself. I told her some things that I have never told anyone before, but I am glad I did."

Maria risked telling Ella many things about herself. The risk could involve being rejected, being ridiculed, or being taken advantage of by Ella. But the risk Maria took was worth it because Ella accepted her. Thus, the first step toward a trusting relationship between these two persons has taken place.

A trusting relationship with someone can also develop when you show that you

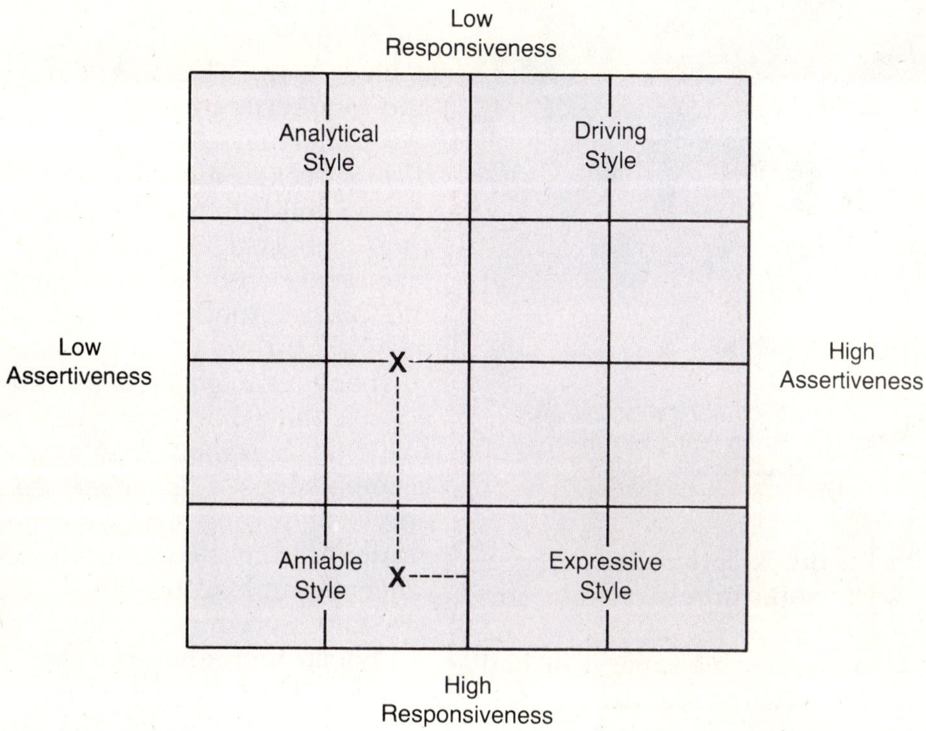


Legend:

| | |
|---|---|
| Driving Style: | determined, demanding, thorough, dominating, pushy |
| Expressive Style: | friendly, stimulating, enthusiastic, excitable, promotable, manipulative |
| Amiable Style: | soft-hearted, accepting, easygoing, complying, retiring |
| Analytical Style: | industrious, persistent, serious, exacting, critical, stuffy |

Each of these personality styles has a backup style. When your usual style isn't working, the following tend to occur: Driviing style becomes a dictator. Expressive style becomes an attacker. Amiable style tends to give in. Analytical style tends to avoid things.



Illus. 2-24. Personality grid.

can be relied upon to get things done. For example, Irving, who was Manuel's supervisor at work, had this to say:

"Manuel surely made our store look good last week. While I was gone, one of our best customers came into the store and was very angry This fellow wanted to know why we hadn't delivered the goods he ordered and demanded to see me. Manuel found this customer's two-week-old order on my desk. It was marked "not in stock." Manuel got right on the phone, called one of our competitors, and filled the order. I am sure Manuel saved this

*Photo by Richard Younker*

Illus. 2-25. Maria builds trusting relationships by taking a risk in telling Ella many things about herself.

account by his quick action. It is a good feeling to know you can rely on your employees."

Manuel knew that his supervisor had confidence in his ability. Manuel justified this confidence by getting the job done in Irving's absence.

## WHERE ARE YOU GOING?

The first four sections of this chapter on self-understanding helped you answer these questions: Who are you? What is important to you? Do you like yourself? Do others like you? This last section will help you answer a final question about yourself: Where are you going?

Successful people and successful businesses know where they are going by setting goals. A *goal* is an objective. It is something you plan to achieve. It gives you purpose and direction in life. An example of a goal at school could be to earn a letter on a varsity team. At work, a goal might be to get high efficiency ratings from your supervisor.

### Short-Term and Long-Term Goals

There are two kinds of goals according to the time span in which you plan to achieve them. These are short-term goals and long-term goals.

A short-term goal could be set for a day, a week, a month. Any objective you can accomplish in a year's time is called a *short-term goal.* An example of a short-term goal could be to get an A grade on this course. Another example could be to have a full-time job this summer.

Long-term goals take more time to achieve than short-term goals. Any objective that takes more than a year's time to accomplish is a *long-term goal.* An example of a long-term goal could be to graduate from a community college. Another example could be to become an assistant store manager in five years.

Short- and long-term goals will help you get ahead in life. You can do more and better things when you set goals. No company ever made a profit without goals. Businesses set goals for 5, 10, and even 15 years ahead. Each year and each month businesses set short-term goals to help reach long-term goals. Businesses do not leave the future to chance. Do you?

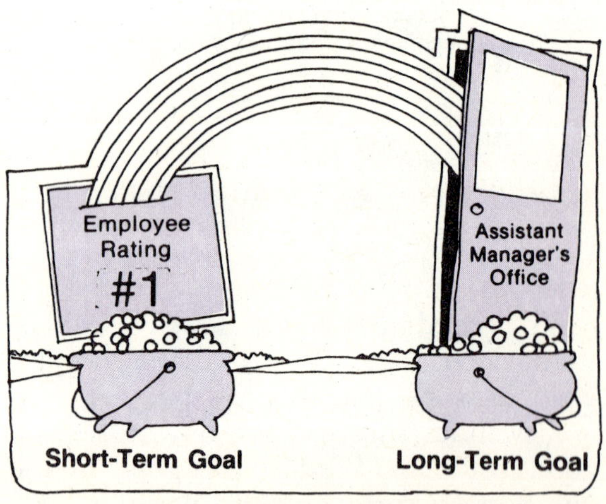


Illus. 2-26. Short-term and long-term.

## Goal-Setting Guidelines

As you plan both types of goals, consider the guidelines given below.

1. *Who owns the goal?* Does the goal belong to you or to someone else? If you set the goal yourself, this means it is yours. Others may give or sell you a goal, but it won't work unless you believe in the goal. When you believe in a goal, you can call the goal your own. The goals you own have a good chance of being accomplished.
2. *Is the goal under your control?* A goal is under your control if the result depends upon your own actions. You are less likely to achieve a goal if you have to depend unnecessarily on somebody's action to accomplish it. Look at the following examples:

### A Goal Dependent on Yourself

I will get to work on time by getting myself up at 7:00 A.M.

On Monday I will ask Cecilia to the dance on Friday night.

### A Goal Dependent on Others

I will get to work on time by having my sister wake me up at 7:00 A.M.

I will let Cecilia know that I want to date her by having Eduardo tell her so.

3. *Is the goal measurable?* How do you know when you reach a goal? If a goal is stated in specific terms, you will know. The more precisely a goal is stated, the easier it is to know when you reach it. Look at the following examples:

### Measurable Goals

I will devote more time to studying by using study periods at school strictly for studying.

I will attend at least half of the home basketball games.

I will join a club or organization that does active things at school.

### Unmeasurable Goals

I will devote more time to studying.

I will get involved in extracurricular activities at school.

4. *Does the goal have a time limit?* Without a specific time limit, a goal is meaningless. In the absence of such a limit, it would be possible to put off achieving the goal. Time limits provide the target date.

### Time Limit

I will save $1,000 over a period of the next 12 months.

I will visit my grandmother on her birthday this year.

### No Time Limit

I will save $1,000.

I will visit my grandmother.

## Priority Setting

You make choices about what to do every day. Some things you must do today. Other things you could do today, tomorrow, or the next day. The process of deciding which things to do today, tomorrow, next week, next month, and so on is called *setting priorities.*

Everyone has written or unwritten lists of things to do. For example, Sam might have the following items on a list of things to do:

- ▶ Studying schoolwork.
- ▶ Working part-time.
- ▶ Making car payments.
- ▶ Going out with friends.
- ▶ Visiting relatives.

A list of things to do becomes a list of priorities when numbers are assigned to the items on the list. Below is Sam's list of priorities:

1. Working part-time.
2. Making car payments.
3. Going out with friends.
4. Studying schoolwork.
5. Visiting relatives.

Note that "studying schoolwork" doesn't rank very high on Sam's list of priorities. His job, car, and friends are more important to him than schoolwork. It is not surprising that at the end of the term Sam's report card showed low grades.

## Changing Priorities

Sometimes it becomes necessary to change priorities. Let us go back to Sam's case and see why he had to change his priorities. Sam's parents were very dis-

Illus. 2-27. Studying is now Sam's top priority.

pleased with his low grades. They told him that if his grades didn't improve during the next term, he would have to quit working. That would mean giving up his car. Sam therefore changed his priorities. Studying is now Sam's top priority. By studying more, Sam will improve his grades. Then he can keep his job and his car and still go out with friends.

## Making Trade-Offs

The process of giving up some things in return for other things is called *making trade-offs.* In order to reach a goal, making trade-offs is often necessary. In Sam's case, for example, he must decrease the amount of time for some things in order to increase his study time—his present goal.

### Sam's Goal

To increase study time by. . . .

### Sam's Alternatives

1. Cutting out TV on weekdays.
2. Staying home on weeknights.
3. Going to school early and studying there.
4. Using study time given in class for studying.

Sam will achieve his goal by taking action on one or more alternatives. Since Sam wants to keep his car, wants to keep his job, and wants to make good grades, he traded off some time for watching TV and some time for going out with friends. In return, Sam had more time for studying.

People in business make trade-offs, too. Successful people in business consider as many alternatives as possible. By doing so, they are ready to make wise decisions and can avoid unwise trade-offs.

# Activity 2-1

## Riddle of the Sphinx

This activity is designed to help you learn more about others. It also gives you the chance to tell about yourself. The title, "Riddle of the Sphinx," comes from the ancient story of *Oedipus Rex* by Sophocles. The riddle, whose answer assured one would not be eaten by the sphinx, is this:

> What in the spring moves on four feet,
> in the summer moves on two feet,
> and in the fall moves on three?
> The more feet it moves, the weaker it be.

Many an unsuccessful traveler guessed nearly every type of animal, bird, or insect. Only Oedipus got it right. If you want to guess, stop here and look away from the page. The answer comes next.

The correct answer to the riddle is the human. We move as babies by crawling on all fours; the reference to spring is to the beginning of life. We move upright on two feet as we mature (our summer). We move on three feet in old age (the fall season); the third foot is a cane or crutch.

*George Bellerose/Stock, Boston*

Illus. 2-28. The Sphinx in Egypt.

Directions:

Draw three pictures in the spaces provided on the next page:

Spring: Picture things that were important to you as a child. What people, places, and things do you see?

Summer: Picture what is important to you as a maturing person. For example, what would your ideal job and ideal vacation be?

Fall: Picture other people asking you for advice. Who are they and what are they asking about? What are you doing?

Artwork isn't important. Make your drawings as brief or as detailed as you wish. Be sure that they contain enough information to answer the questions.

Share your spring, summer, and fall with the class. Explain the meaning of your picture for each season.

This page is for your pictures of your seasons.

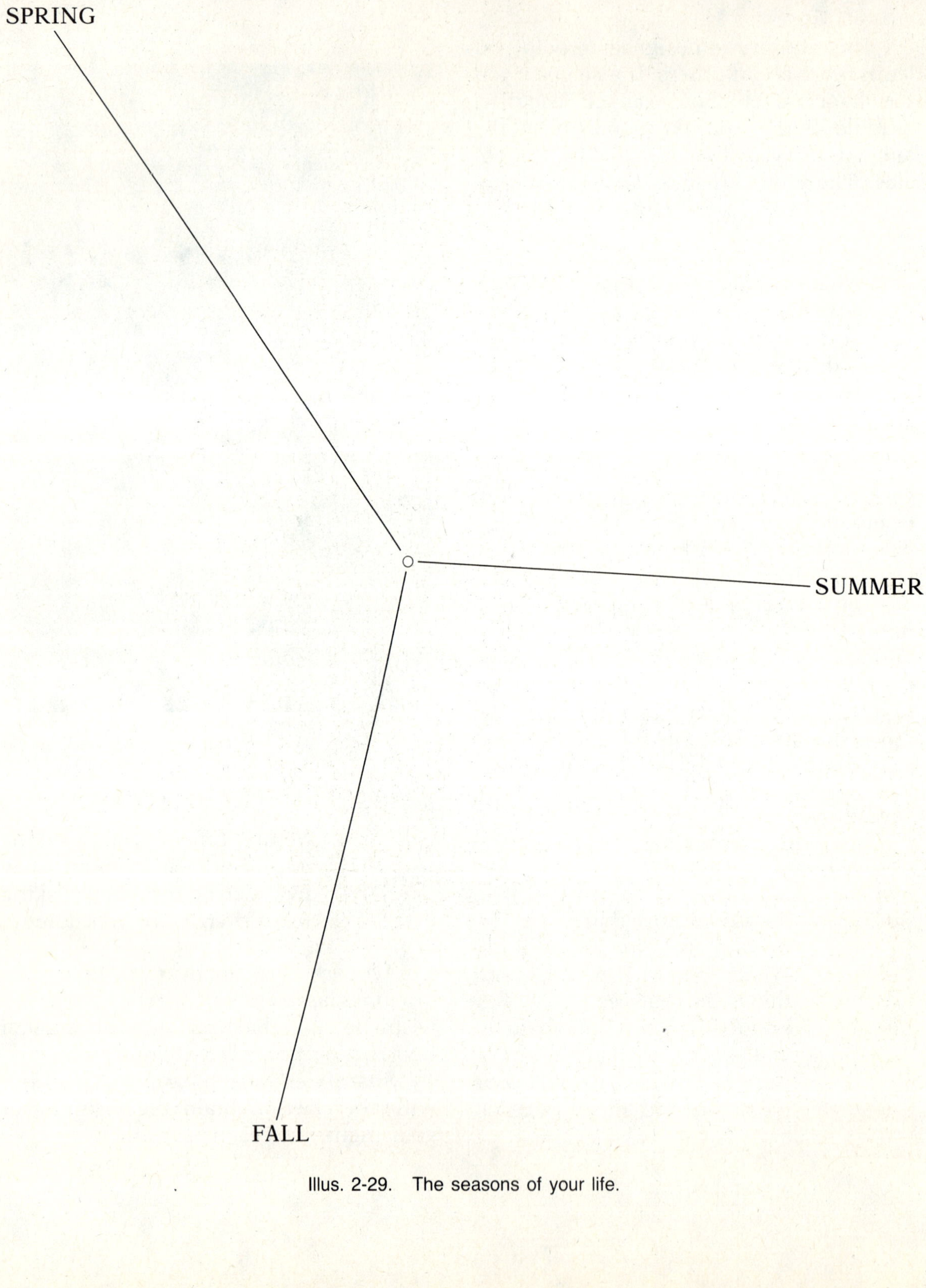


Illus. 2-29. The seasons of your life.

# Activity 2-2

## Methods of Revealing Your Many Selves

The questions in this activity refer to the four methods used to decide which of your many selves to put forward. In the spaces provided, write an answer to each question listed.

1. *Method 1: Doing what others expect.* How can you tell what:

a. Teachers expect?

b. Friends expect?

c. People at work expect?

2. *Method 2: Doing what others prescribe.*

a. What is a prescription? Give an example.

b. Has anyone given you a prescription recently? If so, what was it?

c. Have you given anyone a prescription recently? If so, what was it? Did the person specifically ask for this kind of direction?

d. How do you feel when you get a prescription that you didn't ask for?

e. Do prescriptions help people? Are there dangers in relying on prescriptions?

3. *Method 3: Acting by trial and error.*

a. Do you know anyone like Carlos, the young man in the example on page 24 of this text? If so, describe a way that person uses Method 3.

b. Do students use Method 3 with their parents? If so, give an example.

c. Do parents use Method 3 with each other? If so, give an example.

d. Do employees use Method 3 on their supervisors? If so, give an example.

4. *Method 4: Acting on personal beliefs.*

a. Are people who practice Method 4 inner- or other-directed?

b. What is the main difference between an inner-directed and an other-directed person?

c. What does it mean to be logical and unemotional?

d. Should people be logical and unemotional at all times?

e. How do you know when your actions are based on your personal beliefs?

# Activity 2-3

## The Johari Window

This activity will enable you to plot your own score sheet for your Johari Window. First, follow these directions:

1. Read the words in Columns I and II on this page.

2. Decide which of these words best describe you.

3. Circle the ten words in Column I and the ten words in Column II that best describe you.

4. After you circle the words that best describe you, have three other friends in your class do the same in describing you. Have your friends use Worksheets 2, 3, and 4 on the next three pages.

Worksheet 1: Completed by ______________________________
(your name)

### Words That Best Describe Me

| Column I | Column II |
|---|---|
| accepting | aloof |
| biased | candid |
| critical | clever |
| curious | closemouthed |
| helpful | direct |
| inexperienced | frank |
| innocent | guarded |
| insensitive | noncommittal |
| joking | observant |
| judgmental | obstinate |
| keen | outspoken |
| modest | private |
| nosy | risk-taking |
| persistent | shy |
| questioning | silent |
| receptive | sly |
| searching | straightforward |
| sincere | tactful |
| strong-willed | unselfish |
| trusting | yielding |

Total Points for Column I = _______ Total Points for Column II = _______

Worksheet 2: Completed by ______________________________
(your name)

## Words That Best Describe My Friend

| Column I | Column II |
|---|---|
| accepting | aloof |
| biased | candid |
| critical | clever |
| curious | closemouthed |
| helpful | direct |
| inexperienced | frank |
| innocent | guarded |
| insensitive | noncommittal |
| joking | observant |
| judgmental | obstinate |
| keen | outspoken |
| modest | private |
| nosy | risk-taking |
| persistent | shy |
| questioning | silent |
| receptive | sly |
| searching | straightforward |
| sincere | tactful |
| strong-willed | unselfish |
| trusting | yielding |

Total Points for Column I = _______ Total Points for Column II = _______

Worksheet 3: Completed by ____________________________________________
(your name)

## Words That Best Describe My Friend

| Column I | Column II |
|---|---|
| accepting | aloof |
| biased | candid |
| critical | clever |
| curious | closemouthed |
| helpful | direct |
| inexperienced | frank |
| innocent | guarded |
| insensitive | noncommittal |
| joking | observant |
| judgmental | obstinate |
| keen | outspoken |
| modest | private |
| nosy | risk-taking |
| persistent | shy |
| questioning | silent |
| receptive | sly |
| searching | straightforward |
| sincere | tactful |
| strong-willed | unselfish |
| trusting | yielding |

Total Points for Column I = ________ Total Points for Column II = ________

Worksheet 4: Completed by ______________________________
(your name)

## Words That Best Describe My Friend

| Column I | Column II |
|---|---|
| accepting | aloof |
| biased | candid |
| critical | clever |
| curious | closemouthed |
| helpful | direct |
| inexperienced | frank |
| innocent | guarded |
| insensitive | noncommittal |
| joking | observant |
| judgmental | obstinate |
| keen | outspoken |
| modest | private |
| nosy | risk-taking |
| persistent | shy |
| questioning | silent |
| receptive | sly |
| searching | straightforward |
| sincere | tactful |
| strong-willed | unselfish |
| trusting | yielding |

Total Points for Column I = ________

Total Points for Column II = ________

## Scoring Your Test

1. Your teacher will read the words that receive answer points. Add up the points in each column on the four worksheets. Then place your scores in the spaces provided at the bottom of the worksheets.

2. Illus. 2-29 is an example of a plotted score. In this example the total points are as follows:

### Scores from Worksheet 1

Total Points, Column I = 20
Total Points, Column II = 30

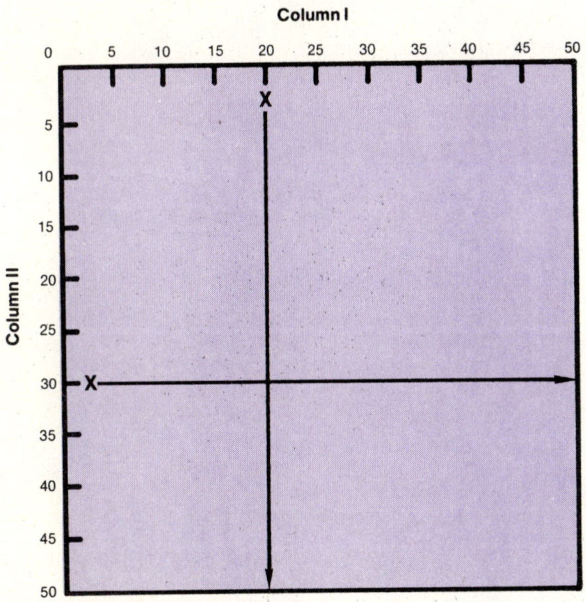


Illus. 2-29. Example of a plotted curve.

The person who plotted Illus. 2-29 would place an X on the top horizontal line by the number 20 in the square and would also place an X by the number 30 on the left vertical line of the square.

3. Plot your score. Then place your X's on the top and left side of the square in Illus. 2-30. Draw your Johari Window by drawing straight lines across the square and down the square.

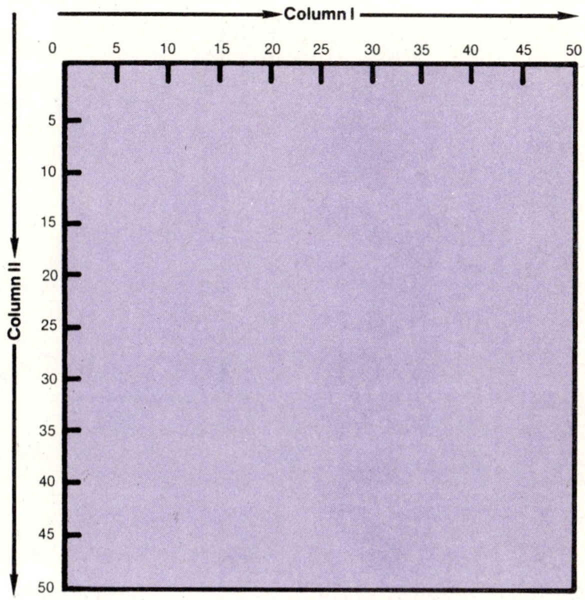


Illus. 2-30. My Johari Window—how I describe myself.

4. Now plot your score in Illus. 2-31 from the three worksheets completed by your three friends. Your score is the sum of the points from each column, divided by 3. For example:

| | Col. I | Col. II |
|---|---|---|
| Scores from Worksheet 2: | 20 | 25 |
| Scores from Worksheet 3: | 15 | 35 |
| Scores from Worksheet 4: | 25 | 30 |
| Total Points | 60 | 90 |
| Total Points Divided by 3 | 60/3 | 90/3 |
| Your Score: | 20 | 30 |

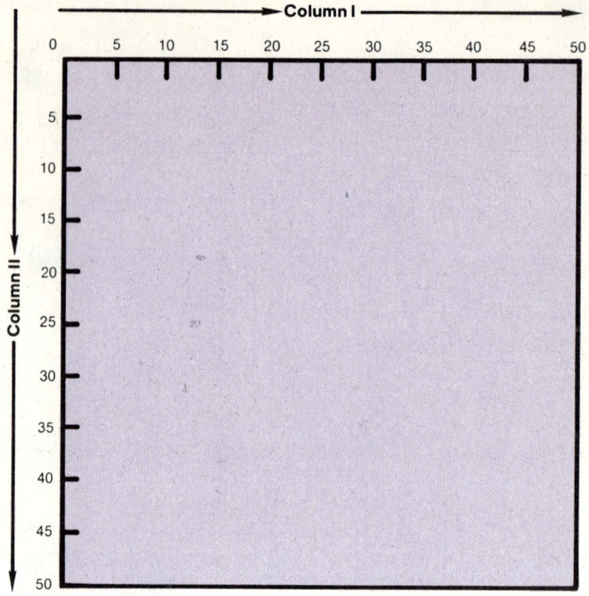


Illus. 2-31. My Johari Window—how others describe me.

## Activity 2-4

### Discussion of the Johari Window

Answer the following questions in the spaces provided.

1. How can a person with a large blind spot decrease the blind spot and increase the arena?

2. How can a person with a large hidden section decrease the hidden section and increase the arena?

3. How can a person with a large unknown section decrease the unknown section and increase the arena?

# Activity 2-5

## Brain Orientation Questionnaire

Read the following statements carefully. Then, using the "Response Key" given below, CIRCLE the responses to the right of the statements that best match your preferences.

### Response Key

SA = strongly agree
A = agree
D = disagree
SD = strongly disagree

| | | | | |
|---|---|---|---|---|
| 1. I am usually on time. | SA | A | D | SD |
| 2. I like to try new fads. | SA | A | D | SD |
| 3. Winning is important. | SA | A | D | SD |
| 4. I like a lot of space. | SA | A | D | SD |
| 5. I prefer to read slowly. | SA | A | D | SD |
| 6. I play a musical instrument. | SA | A | D | SD |
| 7. I am good at math. | SA | A | D | SD |
| 8. I am quick to decide things. | SA | A | D | SD |
| 9. I tend to go back to the same restaurants. | SA | A | D | SD |
| 10. I should be more serious. | SA | A | D | SD |

The Scoring Sheet and directions on how to interpret your score are given below.

### Scoring Sheet

| *Statement #* | *SA* | *A* | *D* | *S* |
|---|---|---|---|---|
| 1 | 1 | 2 | 3 | 3 |
| 2 | 4 | 3 | 2 | 1 |
| 3 | 1 | 2 | 3 | 4 |
| 4 | 4 | 3 | 2 | 1 |
| 5 | 1 | 2 | 3 | 4 |
| 6 | 4 | 3 | 2 | 1 |
| 7 | 1 | 2 | 3 | 4 |
| 8 | 4 | 3 | 2 | 1 |
| 9 | 1 | 2 | 3 | 4 |
| 10 | 4 | 3 | 2 | 1 |

Sum of the numbers circled:______

### Interpret Your Score:

| IF: The total score is | THEN: The dominant brain orientation is: |
|---|---|
| 10 to 20 | Left Brain |
| 21 to 30 | Balanced |
| 31 to 40 | Right Brain |

# Activity 2-6

## Lookout Mountain

A group of tourists went on a sightseeing tour. The tour bus stopped on top of Lookout Mountain. After taking some pictures and walking through some abandoned mine shacks, Cora and her boyfriend, Jim, returned to the bus loading area. The bus was gone. It left accidentally without them. Jim became very upset, for he had left his medicine on the bus. Without the medicine he becomes very ill. In fact, he began to feel ill immediately. Cora wanted to help Jim, so she went to see Lou.

Lou operated the small restaurant on top of the mountain. He owned an old car that Cora hoped he would use to take her to the bus to get Jim's medicine. Lou agreed, provided that Cora would steal the citizen's band radio from the bus for use in his car. Cora refused. She went to Bert, the only other person on the mountain.

Bert was an old miner who lived in a shack behind the restaurant. Cora told him her problem. Bert said he could not help her and that she herself must decide what is right or wrong. Cora decided that she had no choice. She went back to the restaurant. She told Lou she would do as he asked.

When Cora and Lou returned, Cora ran happily to Jim with the medicine. He took it and began to feel better. Then Cora told Jim what she had done. Jim was shocked at her behavior! He told her he never wanted to be seen with her again.

The tour bus returned the next day. While waiting for the bus to leave, Cora told Abe what happened. Abe felt sorry for Cora. Therefore, when Jim came along to get on the bus, Abe grabbed him and beat him up.

1. Rank the people in the story from first place to fifth place in the spaces provided. Assign the first place to the person you like best. Assign the fifth place to the one you like least. Place the other persons in the middle according to how much you like them.

1st place ______________________________

2d place ______________________________

3d place ______________________________

4th place ______________________________

5th place ______________________________

2. Explain why you chose __________ for first place.

______________________________________________

______________________________________________

______________________________________________

3. Which persons are using the "You scratch my back, I'll scratch yours" reasoning? How do you know?

______________________________________________

______________________________________________

______________________________________________

4. Which persons are using punishment as a method of reasoning? How do you know?

______________________________________________

______________________________________________

______________________________________________

5. Did Jim act the way he did because of blind obedience to rules or laws? Explain.

______________________________

______________________________

______________________________

6. Assume that you want to convince someone that Bert should be in first place. What will you say in order to convince that person?

______________________________

______________________________

______________________________

# Activity 2-7

## Time Travel: Values Past, Present, and Future

What were the values of your ancestors? What will be the values of your descendants? What is really important today? This activity will help answer these questions and clarify your own values. The activity is divided into three parts. Your teacher will give you additional directions and help in completing each part.

### Part I: Directions

Ten value items are listed on the next page. Based on your values, which is most important? which is next in importance? Rate the items in this way: give ten points to the most important item, nine points to the next most important item, and so forth, until finally one point is given to the least important item. Write your answers in the "Today" column of the ranking sheet.

### Part II: Directions

This part of the activity will help you get ready to think about the values of the past and the values of the future. Answer the following questions. A written answer is not necessary. Just think of answers and share them in a brief class discussion.

A. 500 Years Ago

1. What were the most common forms of government?
2. What kinds of jobs did people have?
3. What technology (tools) existed to improve the quality of work life and/or personal life?
4. What did people do for entertainment? Where did they go for entertainment?
5. What was the average length of life? Why?

B. 500 Years Ahead

1. What will be the most common forms of government?
2. What kinds of jobs will people have?
3. What technology (tools) will exist to improve the quality of work life and/or personal life?
4. What will people do for entertainment? Where will they go for entertainment?
5. What will be the average length of life? Why?

### Part III

Your teacher will give you directions for completing this part of the activity.

## Time Travel: Value Ranking Sheet

| Item | Today | 500 Years Ago | 500 Years Ahead |
|---|---|---|---|
| Helping sick and disadvantaged people | ________ | ________ | ________ |
| Physical appearance you are proud of | ________ | ________ | ________ |
| Good friends | ________ | ________ | ________ |
| Long, healthy life | ________ | ________ | ________ |
| Happy marriage | ________ | ________ | ________ |
| Freedom for all people | ________ | ________ | ________ |
| Enjoyment of nature and the environment | ________ | ________ | ________ |
| A beautiful home | ________ | ________ | ________ |
| Financial security | ________ | ________ | ________ |

# Activity 2-8

## A Group Dilemma

This activity involves a group discussion problem. Form groups of five people and discuss the following problem:

A nuclear disaster has ended. The only human beings alive are ten people in a bomb shelter. It will take six months for the radiation to drop to a safe level. The supplies in the shelter can barely sustain six people for the six months.

What should they do?

The ten people in the bomb shelter are the following:

1. Susan S., age 60, a history professor.
2. Roe R., age 28, a movie star.
3. Pat K., age 40, a police officer.
4. Kay M., age 21, an Olympic gold medal winner.
5. Lyn P., age 42, a scientist.
6. Marie G., age 34, a physician.
7. Ken B., age 28, a mechanic.
8. Marta B., age 28, the mechanic's pregnant wife.
9. Fr. Jackson, age 36, a priest and civil rights activist.
10. Joe M., age 19, a migrant worker.

Please complete the following statements about the group strategy.

### "I Learned" Statements

1. I learned that I ______________________________
2. I realized that I ______________________________
3. I relearned that I ______________________________
4. I noticed that I ______________________________
5. I discovered that I ______________________________
6. I was surprised that I ______________________________
7. I was displeased that I ______________________________
8. I was pleased that I ______________________________

# Activity 2-9

## Recognizing Strengths

Assume that you are very close to being hired for a job. This job is especially important because it is the *one* job you have been hoping would be offered to you.

The only thing standing between you and this job is a letter of recommendation. You have asked a friend to write this letter. Write the letter to the prospective employer that you would like your friend to write.

**Dear Prospective Employer:**

# Activity 2-10

## Eliminating Fear

Remember how Sara's fears (see page 41) made her a mental wreck on the job? Here is another story about Rex, whose fears get in the way of his performance on the job. Read the following story about Rex. Then answer the questions that follow. Be prepared to discuss your answers in class.

Rex is a part-time sacker at the local grocery store. Rex believes that he is a quiet and shy person. As a result of his belief, Rex rarely talks to the customers or his boss. He is afraid of making mistakes on the job. His boss wonders why Rex spends so much time looking over his shoulder or just fidgeting.

1. Does Rex like himself? Explain your answer.

______________________________

______________________________

______________________________

______________________________

2. What does Rex need to accept about himself?

______________________________

______________________________

______________________________

______________________________

3. Is being quiet and shy a weakness of Rex?

______________________________

______________________________

______________________________

______________________________

4. What are some strong points about being quiet and shy?

______________________________

______________________________

______________________________

______________________________

5. How can Rex build confidence in himself?

______________________________

______________________________

______________________________

______________________________

6. What action can Rex take to eliminate his fears?

______________________________

______________________________

______________________________

______________________________

# Activity 2-11

## The Stress Scale

### Characteristics of Stress-Prone Individuals

Answer these three questions with a "Yes" or "No":

______ 1. Do you have a habit of doing two or three projects at the same time?

______ 2. Do you have a tendency to count things as you work?

______ 3. Are you critical of people who are always late for appointments?

The people who develop stress tests believe that frequent or prolonged stress directly relates to your predicted illness level. It is believed that you can control stress-related illnesses with regular exercise, recreational activities, and a moderate diet.

If you answered yes to all three questions, you may have some of the characteristics of a stress-prone individual. While few of us live without stress, prolonged or excessive stress can have serious physical and mental consequences.

### Strategies for Managing Stress

In the left-hand column, list the behaviors you have observed in yourself or in others that may be stress-related. Use the right-hand column to list at least two actions to manage the stress.

| Stress-Related Behaviors | Strategies for Managing Stress |
|---|---|
| 1.______________________ | 1. a. ______________________ |
| | b. ______________________ |
| 2.______________________ | 2. a. ______________________ |
| | b. ______________________ |
| 3.______________________ | 3. a. ______________________ |
| | b. ______________________ |
| 4.______________________ | 4. a. ______________________ |
| | b. ______________________ |
| 5.______________________ | 5. a. ______________________ |
| | b. ______________________ |

# Activity 2-12

## Trust Walk

Members of the class should form pairs. One person will be the guide for the trust walk. The other will be blindfolded. The guide takes the hand or arm of the "blind" partner through an obstacle course in the room. Points are earned by making it around the barriers. As a group, you decide on the barriers and the points. Switch roles after one partner is led through the course.

An alternative for this activity is to omit the points and walk around the building.

After the "trust walk," in the spaces provided answer the questions listed below.

1. Did you trust your guide at first? Explain your answer.

_______________________________________

_______________________________________

_______________________________________

_______________________________________

_______________________________________

2. Did you trust your guide near the end of the trust walk? Explain your answer.

_______________________________________

_______________________________________

_______________________________________

_______________________________________

_______________________________________

3. How did it feel to depend on someone?

_______________________________________

_______________________________________

_______________________________________

_______________________________________

4. How did it feel to have someone depend on you?

_______________________________________

_______________________________________

_______________________________________

_______________________________________

5. What did you learn about your guide when you were led around?

_______________________________________

_______________________________________

_______________________________________

_______________________________________

6. What did you learn about your "blind" partner as you led this person around?

_______________________________________

_______________________________________

_______________________________________

# Activity 2-13

## Taking Risks

Trust develops when you risk being open about yourself with others. Try completing the following sentences as openly and honestly as you can. You may choose not to complete some sentences, for that is your right.

1. I am most comfortable when I

___

___

2. I worry most about

___

___

3. I like to spend my free time on

___

___

4. I like/don't like certain people because

___

___

5. I believe/don't believe in something I am told because

___

___

6. I agree/don't agree with my friends when they say

___

___

7. Even though my friends don't agree, I like to

___

___

8. I like/don't like people who

___

___

9. I admire others who

___

___

10. I get angry with others when they

___

___

Now go back over your statements. Which of these beliefs and feelings are you willing to tell others? Which can you tell a close friend, the people you work with, your supervisor, or your parents? Which statements are you unwilling to reveal even to a close friend? Read the following questions and think about your answers as you read these questions.

1. Why is it considered risky to reveal personal beliefs?

___

___

___

___

2. Do you know people who ridicule others when these others share their personal beliefs?

______________________________________

______________________________________

______________________________________

______________________________________

3. How can you take risks in revealing yourself to others without fearing rejection or ridicule by them?

______________________________________

______________________________________

______________________________________

______________________________________

4. Which of the statements on page 81 would you now risk revealing to a close friend?

______________________________________

______________________________________

______________________________________

______________________________________

5. Does your own trust increase when you risk telling others about yourself?

______________________________________

______________________________________

______________________________________

______________________________________

Share your answer to Question 3 in class. What kinds of help have others in the class suggested?

# Activity 2-14

## Life Lines

Follow these directions:

1. In the space below, draw a horizontal line. Let the line represent your past, present, and future.

2. Place an X on the line to show where you are today.

3. Place a Y on the line to represent where you expect to be five years from now.

4. On the bottom of this page, write a description of yourself as you see yourself five years from now.

5. Write a long-term goal for yourself.

6. Write three short-term goals that will help you reach the long-term goal you just wrote. Be sure your goals are measurable.

# Activity 2-15

## Priorities and Trade-Offs

1. What are priorities?

2. List your priorities for this week.

3. Write three examples of trade-offs that you or someone you know chose to make.

4. How do trade-offs differ from quitting?

Chapter 3

# Teamwork

KNOWLEDGE: After reading this chapter, you will be able to:

1. Analyze the concept of being accepted by co-workers.
2. Compare and contrast written and unwritten rules.
3. Describe the process of making assumptions.
4. State reasons why people are unwilling to ask questions.
5. Describe common impositions of employees on co-workers.
6. Analyze the concept of tolerance by defining tolerance and by describing ways in which to increase tolerance.
7. State reasons why people want to get ahead in life.
8. Describe positive and negative aspects of flattery.
9. List guidelines for getting ahead while getting along with co-workers.

ATTITUDES: After reading this chapter, you will:

1. Believe that the main reason people lose jobs is because they are unable to get along with others at work.
2. Value the ability to accept the differing life-styles of others.
3. Gain satisfaction from the knowledge that appearance and attitude are important aspects of being accepted by co-workers.
4. Value written and unwritten rules.
5. Make an effort to ask questions when trying to find out what is expected.
6. Recognize the importance of the time element in work breaks and in arriving at and leaving from work.
7. Value the ability to show tolerance for others.
8. Value the importance of getting along with co-workers while advancing in a career.

People work for many reasons. Some people work in paid jobs, others work in volunteer organizations, and still others work at home in unpaid jobs. A definition of a *good job* is one where you value what you do and you like the people you work with. People who value their work believe that what they do is important. Here *important* means that the job helps develop or deliver a product or a service.

The second part of the definition of a good job—liking the people you work with or people who are on your team—also implies that you are liked by those same people. Certainly everyone at work does not necessarily like everyone else. This is when human relations becomes important. Your ability to get along with co-workers, whether you like them or not, is often the difference between being unemployed or employed. It amounts to being a good team member.

Those who study reasons why people either leave or lose their jobs have found that there is one main reason. Usually it is *not* because a worker does not know how to do the job. Instead, the main reason is that many people have a hard time getting along with their co-workers. As a future employee in any organization, one of the most important skills you can learn is how to get along with other employees. If you can learn how to get along with your co-workers, you are well on your way to becoming a good team member and employee in any kind of job.

## BEING ACCEPTED

Being accepted in a job by co-employees means that others like you as a co-worker. They listen to you when you talk with them. They like you for yourself and welcome you into the organization. Being accepted by others is the first step in getting along in any work environment.

Everyone wants to be accepted, and being accepted is especially important to employees. It is important because the worker who does not feel acceptable to others is usually unhappy and is not very

Illus. 3-1. People who value their work believe that what they do is important.

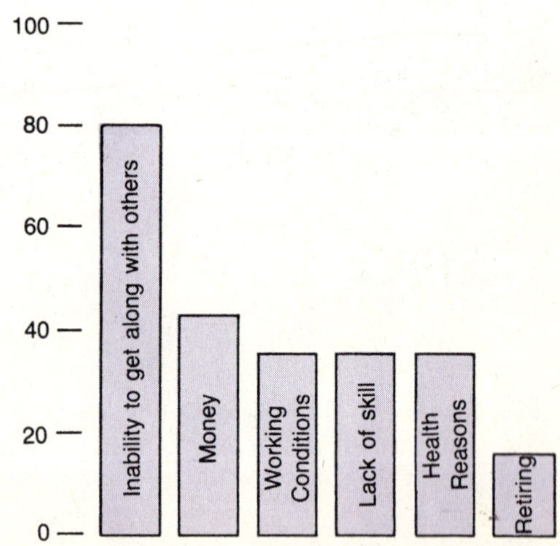


Illus. 3-2. Reasons why people leave jobs.

productive. On the other hand, one who feels accepted by other people at work is more likely to be a happy and satisfied worker. Happy and satisfied workers tend to keep their jobs. They get raises in pay, promotions, and other special recognition from their employers.

Being accepted by co-workers may take some time, but you can speed up things by using several techniques. Some of the more important techniques are: (1) learning to accept others' life-styles, (2) trying not to make incorrect assumptions, (3) maintaining a good appearance, and (4) developing a good attitude. If you do these things, other workers at your job will recognize and accept you as a person with whom they want to work.

## Accept Other People's Life-Styles

The ways in which people live are called *life-styles.* Life-styles can include people's beliefs, eating habits, housing, education, leisure activities, manner of dressing, and many other daily activities. There are hundreds of different life-styles, and several of them probably will be represented where you work. The idea, of course, is to respect the way others choose to live and behave. One need never make fun of another's speech, dress, religion, home, eating habits, ideas, or beliefs. It is important to respect another person's right to be different.

When you respect others, this quality about you will be quickly noticed. It will

Illus. 3-3. When you are willing to accept others, they will tend to accept you, too.

help you to be accepted in any organization. It is also well to remember that accepting other people's life-styles is usually a two-way street. When you are willing to accept others, they will tend to accept you, too.

## Avoid Incorrect Assumptions

Another technique you can learn to help you become accepted in any organization is closely related to accepting others' life-styles. It involves the art of learning not to make incorrect assumptions about people. Making an incorrect assumption means making a judgment without the facts.

For example, you might assume that a person has difficulty speaking English because that person comes from a foreign country, or you might assume that a person is poor because of his or her manner of dressing. People are often offended by incorrect assumptions made about them. This makes for poor human relations. Avoiding incorrect assumptions about people can help you find greater acceptance in any organization.

## Maintain a Good Appearance

Appearance can affect your chances for acceptance at work. Remember that *you make a first impression only once.* You will improve your ability to make a good impression if you are:

- *Alert*—head up, smiling, and looking people in the eye.[1]
- *Natural*—using common language when talking with people and not trying to impress them with slang or technical terms.
- *Distinct*—speaking clearly without muttering, and using an appropriate voice inflection with a moderate pace.
- *Pleasant*—using the other person's name while speaking to him or her, ending with a "pleasure to meet you" or "hope to see you again" remark, and delivering these phrases with sincerity.

Illus. 3-4. Give some thought to your clothes and grooming before you start a new job.

[1]Note that good eye contact means giving the other person about the same amount of eye contact that he or she gives you.

A good first impression will help you on your way to being accepted.

Give some thought to your clothes and grooming before you start a new job. First, make certain you are clean and neat; that is, teeth brushed, hair combed, body bathed. Also make certain you are appropriately dressed. A good time to learn how to dress for a job is when you are applying for it. Notice how others are dressed for work, and try to wear clothes resembling theirs. Don't overdress or underdress; that is, your clothing shouldn't be too dressy or too casual for the job. Whether it is right or wrong, you'll be surprised to find that many people decide to accept or reject others based on their appearances.

## Develop a Good Attitude

Perhaps the greatest factor that determines one's acceptance by others in any work environment is attitude. Your work attitude shows how you feel and act about your job and your co-workers. Co-workers are usually more willing to accept a person who has a good attitude.

Having a good attitude can mean many things. It means willingness to work hard and to be ambitious. It means trying to be pleasant to others, as well as

Illus. 3-5. Your clothing shouldn't be too dressy or too casual for the job.

trying to be courteous and respectful to those with whom you work. This means that you avoid being a know-it-all or having a chip on your shoulder. Finally, having a good attitude tells people you care about others on your work team.

## OBSERVING RULES

Most employers have a set of written rules for employees to follow. In every company you will also discover that there are *unwritten* rules that employees are expected to follow. Observing these rules results in better human relations and helps to make an organization run more smoothly. By following both written and unwritten rules, you will learn to get along better with your co-workers.

### Written Rules

Many employers prepare handbooks of rules for their employees. Employee handbooks are different from one organization to another, but they contain similar kinds of information. For example, these handbooks will state what the working hours are and what the policies are concerning vacation, sick leave, and work breaks.

Employee handbooks also list rules and suggestions in several other areas. Handbooks may tell how commissions from certain sales are to be divided among employees. Handbooks list lunch and dinner hours and rules about use of the employees' lounge. They also state in what parts of the building other activities are permitted.

Organizations in which employees are represented by a labor union have a written set of rules referred to as the *contract*. The contract is the collective bargaining agreement between the organization and the employees. It is a legal contract and is enforced by law. The contract contains rules and procedures covering such items as:

- work schedules.
- pay.
- length of vacations.
- days off from work or holidays.
- death and disability benefits.
- layoff procedures.
- grievance procedures.

As a new employee, you will have much greater success getting along with your co-workers if you will read and follow carefully your company's handbook for employees.

### Unwritten Rules

In almost every organization you will find that unwritten rules exist. Even though these rules are not in writing, you will be expected to follow them if you want to get along with co-workers. How can you find out what these unwritten rules are, and how important they are? Most unwritten rules are based on three factors: (1) the seniority system, (2) territorial rights, and (3) consideration.

Illus. 3-6. Learn your company's written rules and follow them.

### *The Seniority System*

*Seniority* on the job involves the length of time a person has been employed by an organization. For example, a person who has worked for an organization for ten years would have more seniority than one who has worked there for only two years.

In many organizations people with the most seniority enjoy certain privileges. For example, they may be allowed to take their work breaks first. They may be given the first chance to work overtime for extra pay when there is extra work to be done. Or they may be the first to choose from a scheduled vacation time if there is one.

For unionized employees, most seniority privileges are written into the contract.

*Mimi Forsyth/Monkmeyer Press*

Illus. 3-7. In many organizations people with the most seniority may be allowed to choose their vacation times first.

Some examples of these privileges are concerned with the items that were listed in the previous section about written rules. In nonunion organizations, the seniority system is usually based on tradition and is not in writing. In either situation—union or nonunion—a healthy respect for the rules of seniority will help you get along with others at work.

### *Territorial Rights*

Territorial rights are something like seniority, and they are often established over a period of time. These are rights of a person who controls a certain area, or territory. When you are in a territory controlled by another person, you are generally expected to respect the wishes of that person.

For example, in the restaurant business, an unwritten rule involving territorial rights for waiters or waitresses may be to wait on customers only in designated areas. It is important to know the "territory" of your work situation. Some major department stores have begun an "inter-selling" policy by which salespeople are expected to sell in several departments. Other stores may have more strictly defined areas. For example, a salesperson in the lingerie department may not be welcome in the sportswear department.

Sometimes territorial rights are hard to understand. One way to help understand these rights is to think about some territory that you consider to be your own. For example, you may have your own room, some special chest of drawers, or a special chair. You may become very uncomfortable when someone takes over your own area or areas. Remembering this feeling may help you respect others' territories on the job and

*Photo courtesy of Perkins Restaurants*

Illus. 3-8. It is important to know the "territory" of your work situation.

may help promote human relations at work.

### *Consideration*

One of the most important unwritten rules is to be considerate toward those people with whom you work. Being considerate means many things. It can mean helping someone who suddenly gets very busy. It can mean helping someone lift a heavy box. It could also mean asking permission to use a co-worker's tool. Being considerate of others includes thinking before you act. If you are considerate of others, you will find that you can get along better with them.

## CARRYING YOUR OWN WEIGHT

In order to get along with others on a work team, it is important to do your share of the work. In this section you will learn: (1) how to ask questions so that you can find out what is expected of you and (2) what you are expected *not* to do. To get along with your co-workers, you must carry your own weight.

### Ask Questions

To do a good job, you must know what is expected of you. The best way to learn is to ask questions. Some people do not ask many questions, and as a result they may not learn very fast. These people may even do things in a wrong way rather than ask questions. The biggest reason some employees don't ask questions is *fear*—they are afraid to ask! Why are they afraid?

Let's look at some examples. Thelma wasn't sure how to complete a charge sale on the cash register. When a customer wanted to charge the cost of a group's lunch tickets on a credit card, Thelma really got nervous. Because she wanted to do it just right, Thelma asked her supervisor, Ms. Lopez, "Would you help me with this charge sale?" Ms. Lopez answered, "Thelma, you should know that! How many more times do I have to show you how to do this?" Then Ms. Lopez looked at Thelma's customer, frowned, and shook her head. Thelma was embarrassed. She was ridiculed for asking a question. Do you think she will ask Ms. Lopez many more questions?

Another example is Larry, who did not ask questions because he was afraid that other people would think he was not very smart. Larry worried about this because he was not good at spelling. Whenever he had to write an invoice for a sale to a customer, he panicked because he was not sure how to spell some of the items. Rather than ask about the correct spelling, he left some of the spaces blank and misspelled other words. In other sections of the invoice, he tried to cover up by writing so badly that no one, including himself, could read what he wrote. The bookkeeper had to call Larry in to the office and ask him what the items on the invoice were. When Larry couldn't remember, the bookkeeper had to look up the items by their stock numbers. Larry did not carry his own weight, and the bookkeeper had to carry some of it for him. As a result, Larry had a more difficult time getting along with others. He created extra work for others by being afraid to ask questions.

Illus. 3-10. Larry would rather misspell than ask or look up the correct spelling.

Illus. 3-9. Consideration can mean asking permission to use a co-worker's tool or equipment.

What can you do if you are afraid to ask questions? Here are some ways to get over the fear of asking questions:

1. *Feel good about yourself before you ask.* If you know you have been working hard to learn your job, then you will feel more comfortable asking questions. Knowing that you are giving 100 percent to

the job makes you feel good inside. Then, when you ask a question, it is about something you honestly don't know. Sincerity in asking questions makes other people want to help you.

2. *Ask someone you trust.* Find someone at work whom you like and think you can trust. Tell that person you need to ask questions to learn what you are supposed to do. When you are honest with someone and ask for help, it makes that person feel good. When you ask people for help, you make them feel important and needed.
3. *Face a person who ridicules you—privately.* Do you remember how Thelma felt when she was embarrassed by Ms. Lopez? The best way to clear the air is by a private discussion. Facing up to someone who embarrassed you is very difficult, but the payoff is great. However, actions like this need to be made privately. As soon as you have the opportunity, talk to the person and explain your double embarrassment: (1) you were embarrassed by your mistake, and (2) you were embarrassed by the way in which you were corrected. Explain that you want and need help, and ask the person to continue giving you help. The best approach is one of sincerity.

## Don't Impose on Others

Carrying your own weight means more than being good at what you're doing. It also means not imposing on coworkers. Some employees impose on others by (1) calling in sick when they don't feel like working, (2) taking extra long

Illus. 3-11. Here is an employee abusing sick leave.

work breaks, (3) failing to cooperate, and (4) coming to work late and leaving early.

### *Abusing Sick Leave*

Most employers have sick-leave policies described in their employee handbooks. Sick leave is a benefit that allows an employee to be absent from work because of illness. In many cases full-time employees who miss work still get paid for the days they were absent because of illness. Some employees are not ill very often. However, because they use very few sick days, they may feel as if their employer owes them something. As a result, these people may use sick days for one-day vacations. They call in sick when they are well but simply don't want to work that day. This is wrong for two important reasons. First, such employees are cheating their employer. Second, they are also cheating their co-workers. When a worker calls in sick, everyone else on the team has to pitch in and do this absent employee's work.

### *Extending Work Breaks*

In most organizations, work breaks are scheduled. When some employees are in the lounge area during work breaks, others are usually working. One sure and fast way to upset co-workers is to take a long break. If employees extend their work breaks beyond the limit, this upsets the break schedules.

For example, employees who are supposed to get a break at 10:00 don't like to wait until 10:30 just because others have not yet returned from their breaks. Ask yourself, How would I feel if other workers got longer breaks than I? You probably would not be very happy. When you work, be considerate and take only the

Illus. 3-12. These employees are extending their work break and upsetting other employees.

time you're entitled to take on work breaks.

### *Failing to Cooperate*

Doing your share of the work sometimes means helping others on your team. Make every effort to be a team player. When someone has a bad day, make an extra effort to help. Everyone has days or times when he or she does not feel just right. This may happen to you. When it does, your co-workers will also help. Carrying your own weight sometimes means carrying a bit of someone else's.

### *Being a LIFO (Last In, First Out)*

Being the *L*ast *I*n to work and the *F*irst one *O*ut means coming to work at the last possible minute and leaving at the earliest possible time. Being a LIFO can cause poor human relations. Your co-

Illus. 3-13. Going to work a little early shows everyone that you like your job.

workers may get the feeling that you're not interested in working there. Here is a tip that will make you a better co-worker: Get to work a little early and leave on time. When you come early, it gives you a chance to relax before work and to talk with other employees. This little bit of extra effort can be very important. Getting to work early shows everyone that you like your job and that you are eager to begin work.

## DEVELOPING TOLERANCE

You have learned that getting along with co-workers depends on being accepted, following written and unwritten rules, and carrying your own weight. In this section you will learn about being tolerant of others' habits or mannerisms. You will learn: (1) the meaning of tolerance levels and (2) how to increase your tolerance.

Many good working relationships fail to develop because one person will not tolerate another's habits or mannerisms. For example, you may find some of a person's habits or mannerisms irritating. Some habits or mannerisms that might irritate others include:

- Unusual voice or laughter.
- Bragging.
- Complaining.
- Gossiping.
- Using the same expressions or words constantly.
- Using vulgar language.
- Combing hair frequently.

Unfortunately, many people do not realize that they have these habits. Furthermore, they have no idea that others find these habits or mannerisms annoying. If you try to be tolerant of the irritating habits of your co-workers, you will get along with them much better.

### Tolerance Levels

The point at which others' habits or mannerisms begin to bother you is called your *tolerance level.* Your tolerance level constantly changes. In some ways your tolerance level is like a window. On good days the window is open and very little bothers you; you can take in a lot. However, on bad days the window is closed, and there is no room inside for anything. As you might expect, your tolerance level is high on good days and low on bad ones.

Your tolerance level is very complex. It is affected by things that make you hap-

Illus. 3-14. Do irritating habits bother you?

py and by things that make you sad. Your appearance or even the amount of sleep you had the night before can affect your tolerance level. In the same way, a flat tire on your car, a grumpy friend, or even the weather can influence your level of tolerance. While your appearance and amount of sleep are matters over which you may have control, you have no control over a grumpy friend, someone throwing a nail in the street, or the weather. Thus, your level of tolerance is determined by two kinds of things: (1) those you can control and (2) those you cannot control.

## Increasing Your Tolerance Level

The more tolerant you are, the better you will get along with your co-workers. When you have a high tolerance level, the habits or mannerisms of others don't easily bother you. Before you can increase your tolerance level, however, you must recognize the things you cannot control. These things can be very upsetting, but they happen to everyone and there is not much you can do to change them. If you worry about things you cannot control, you usually lose energy because worrying takes energy. When you lose energy, your tolerance goes down. The best thing you can do is to recognize things you cannot control. Then keep going. Things you have no control over can only shut your tolerance window as tight as you let them.

Once you recognize the things you cannot control, you can increase your tolerance level by exercising power over the things you can control in a given situation. You can exercise this power by taking the following steps: (1) separate the irritating behavior from the person, (2) identify your direct and indirect alternatives, and (3) solve the problem by choosing the best direct alternative. These steps will be illustrated by the problem of Don, who had a low tolerance for people who brag.

### *Separate the Behavior from the Person*

Don could not tolerate the way a co-worker, Bob, was always bragging. It was

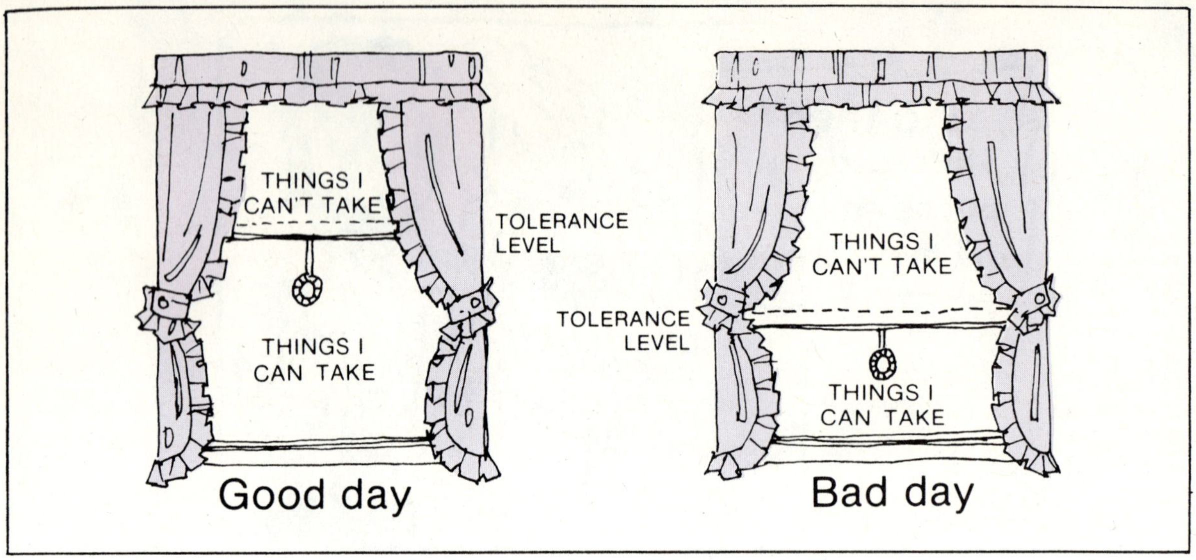


Illus. 3-15. Tolerance windows.

a bad situation because Bob and Don had to work together. Don knew it was important that they get along; however, the situation seemed to be getting worse. Don dreaded each day at work with Bob since he had to listen to Bob brag constantly. Don believed that he had done everything he could to increase his tolerance level, but Bob forced Don's tolerance window closed merely by his presence.

At first Don was ready to quit. However, he decided to take the first step in solving the problem by learning to separate the irritating behavior from the person. Don believed he could like Bob if Bob didn't brag so much. Bragging was the problem, not Bob himself. After all, Bob did a lot of things Don liked. For example, Bob carried his own weight at work. And when Don's car was in the repair shop, it was Bob who first offered him rides home.

### *Identify Direct and Indirect Alternatives*

Next, Don asked himself, "Now that I have separated the behavior from the person, what do I do?" Don considered asking some of the other employees to do something for him. He thought about asking Lois to talk to Bob, since he thought Lois might subtly explain the problem and ask Bob to stop the bragging. This kind of action, which depends upon others for results, is called an *indirect alternative.* As a general rule, indirect alternatives don't solve problems. Before asking others to do something for you, consider these thoughts: They may not do the task the way you want it done. They may make a half-hearted effort. They may not do the task as quickly as you would like it done.

Don decided it would be better to do something himself. Those things you do for yourself are called *direct alternatives.* The best way to solve a problem is through direct alternatives, since you have the greatest amount of control over direct alternatives. Don thought over his direct alternatives. They were:

1. Face Bob and have it out with him.

Illus. 3-16. Here is Bob bragging to Don.

2. Don't respond to Bob when he brags.
3. Change the subject when Bob starts to brag.
4. Excuse himself and leave the area when Bob starts to brag.
5. Avoid Bob by staying away from him whenever possible.

### *Choose the Best Direct Alternative*

In the space provided below, write down what you think is Don's best direct alternative. Then explain your choice.

______________________________

______________________________

______________________________

______________________________

______________________________

______________________________

## GETTING AHEAD WHILE GETTING ALONG

Getting ahead means different things to different people. To some people it means more money. To others it means recognition for a job well done. Yet some people see getting ahead as a *win-or-lose* situation. They think only winners advance, and losers stay behind. You will now explore (1) why people want to get ahead, (2) what people say and do to get ahead, and (3) how you can get ahead while getting along with co-workers on your team.

### Why People Want to Get Ahead

There are hundreds of reasons why people work. But most of these reasons are related to three basic factors: (1) money, (2) recognition, and (3) personal satisfaction.

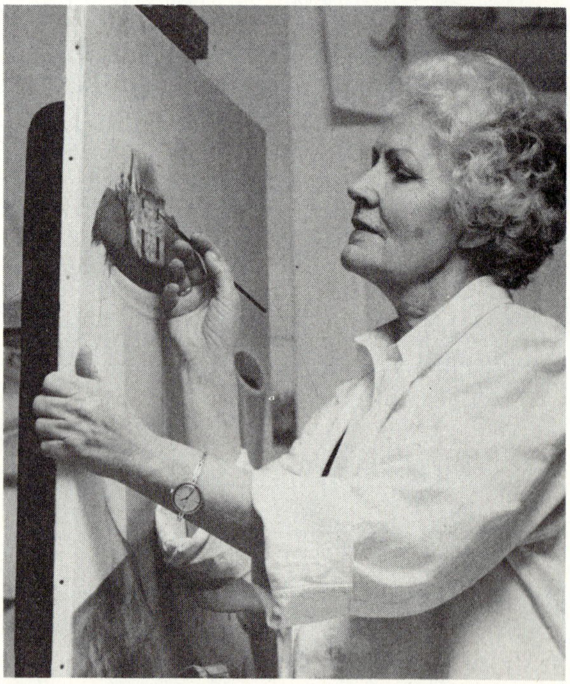

*Zefa/H. Armstrong Roberts*

Illus. 3-17. There are different reasons for wanting to get ahead.

### *Money*

When you have no money, or very little of it, money can be the most important reason to work. But when you have enough to buy most of the things you want, other reasons become more important.

### *Recognition*

Being recognized, rather than money, can be the most important reason to work. This was demonstrated by workers at one company. A few hundred assembly-line workers and their supervisors were asked: "What is most important to you?" In their responses, recognition was first; money was second.

An advancement or promotion usually means more responsibility. In some ways an advancement means getting both recognition and money. In order to be promoted, you must be recognized for doing a good job. And when you are promoted, you usually get more money.

### *Personal Satisfaction*

Personal satisfaction is a result of enjoying the work you do. It is a feeling inside of you that is a sense of pride or accomplishment. This special feeling is present most of the time for those who are in a job they like. Some people rarely get this feeling. They are in jobs where the work is just work. They don't dislike the job, nor do they like it. For such individuals, getting ahead at work is unlikely to happen.

## What People Say and Do to Get Ahead

There is a right way and a wrong way to do almost anything. Getting along with co-workers while earning more money, receiving recognition, and achieving personal satisfaction is the right way. Yet some people want recognition so badly that they forget about human relations. Other people simply never learn how to get ahead while getting along. Employees who don't care or never learn about the right way to get ahead can cause problems. Helen's promotion is a case in point.

Helen wanted to become the new assistant manager of a small printing shop. She thought she had a good chance for the promotion because the manager had complimented her several times for her good work. But there were Vincent and Rose, who were her most likely rivals for the job. So, Helen began to make a point of flattering the manager and saying unkind things about Vincent and Rose to other workers. For example, Helen would say: "I wonder how often Vincent gets a haircut," or "My, isn't Rose wearing an old-fashioned dress!" When some of Helen's nasty comments got back to Vincent and Rose, naturally they became upset.

Helen wanted to be a *winner.* She tried to make Vincent and Rose losers. All her flattering remarks about the manager were made with her own self-interest in mind. Helen may get ahead, but she certainly isn't getting along with her co-workers.

## Tips on Getting Ahead While Getting Along

Getting along with co-workers on your team should be one of your highest priorities. Here are some tips to help you get along while getting ahead:

1. *Accept praise gracefully.* When the manager praises you, look her or

him in the eyes and say, "Thank you." Don't put yourself down by saying things like "Oh, anybody could have done it." Resist the urge to tell other employees about your personal success. Allow the manager or a co-worker who might know about your efforts to brag about you.

2. *Share the credit.* Sometimes you receive praise for the efforts of yourself and others. If you do receive credit for doing a job in which others have helped you, share the credit. Accept thanks for your part, but be sure to tell about the efforts of others.
3. *Flatter people sincerely.* Individuals like to hear nice things said about themselves. When you flatter someone, do it because you want to do it. Don't do it because you feel obligated to flatter. To flatter someone because that person can help advance your career is a big mistake.
4. *Don't flaunt special privileges.* As you get ahead, you are given more responsibility. As you assume more responsibility, you will receive some benefits or privileges. You may be given your own desk or you may be assigned special work. When these privileges are given to you, accept them quietly. Don't wave them in front of your co-workers. You have the right to be proud, but resist showing off to your fellow employees.
5. *Let everyone be a winner.* Getting ahead does not mean getting ahead of someone else at any cost. It means getting yourself ahead without putting others down. Putting yourself up by putting others down is a weakness. No one has to be a loser to make another person a winner. If you see your fellow employees as losers, they may try to make you a loser. But if you see them and yourself as winners, you will get along with your fellow team members.

# Activity 3-1

## Making Assumptions

While reading this chapter, you learned that making incorrect assumptions about people can sometimes lead to difficulty. This activity requires you to make some assumptions about the situations in Illus. 3-18a and 3-18b. Fill in the balloons with some words that you think fit the people in the illustrations. After you have filled in the balloons, below each illustration list the assumptions you made about the situations *before* you filled in the balloons with words. Then discuss your assumptions with others.

Illus. 3-18a. Making assumptions.

Illus. 3-18b. Making assumptions.

# Activity 3-2

## Identifying Written and Unwritten Rules

Just like business firms, schools have written and unwritten rules. Either by yourself or as a class, try to write down briefly some of the written and unwritten rules that exist in your school. Then discuss the questions.

### Written Rules

______________________________

______________________________

______________________________

______________________________

______________________________

______________________________

### Unwritten Rules

______________________________

______________________________

______________________________

______________________________

______________________________

______________________________

1. Which rules are easier to learn? Why?

______________________________

______________________________

______________________________

______________________________

2. How can the unwritten rules be discovered?

______________________________

______________________________

______________________________

______________________________

3. Who makes the written rules? The unwritten rules?

______________________________

______________________________

______________________________

______________________________

4. Are the consequences for violating a written rule worse than for violating an unwritten rule? Why?

______________________________

______________________________

______________________________

______________________________

5. Do you think your school's written and unwritten rules are like those of a business firm or other workplace?

______________________________

______________________________

______________________________

______________________________

# Activity 3-3

## Asking Questions

Learning to ask questions in a new situation is an important skill. This activity will give you some practice in developing that skill. Follow these directions:

1. Your teacher will select two students in your class to role-play a business situation. One student will take the role of manager, and another will take the role of a *new* employee. The new employee may ask for more directions or additional information at any point during the role-playing.
2. The rest of the students in your class should write down the instructions given by the "manager" to the "new employee" in the spaces provided below.

### Instructions from the Manager

________________________________

________________________________

________________________________

________________________________

3. After the role-playing, the person playing the new employee should repeat as many of the instructions as he or she can remember. The new employee may not ask for any new information at this point.
4. The rest of the students should write in the spaces in Table 3-1 what the new employee heard. Did the new employee leave out any instructions (omissions)? Did the new employee substitute one instruction for another (substitutions)? Did the new employee confuse any of the instructions given by the manager (distortions)?

As a class, discuss the following questions:

1. Did the person playing the manager's role give clear instructions?
2. Did the person playing the new employee ask any questions? What were they?
3. Did the new employee get all of the instructions right? If not, what information was left out, substituted, or confused?
4. Why is it important to ask questions if something isn't understood?

| Omissions | Substitutions | Distortions |
|---|---|---|
| | | |
| | | |
| | | |
| | | |
| | | |
| | | |

Table 3-1. What the new employee heard.

# Activity 3-4

## Gripe List

This activity may help you let off some steam and at the same time help you learn something about the tolerance of others. Take a pencil and, in the spaces provided, write out your personal "gripe list." Write down all those habits and mannerisms about others that bother you, especially on *bad days*.

### Facial and Bodily Mannerisms

*Example:* annoying gestures

______________________________

______________________________

______________________________

______________________________

______________________________

### Speech and Language

*Example:* overused words

______________________________

______________________________

______________________________

______________________________

______________________________

### Voice Sounds and Tones

*Example:* high-pitched voice

______________________________

______________________________

______________________________

______________________________

______________________________

### Dress and Appearance

*Example:* dirty fingernails

______________________________

______________________________

______________________________

______________________________

______________________________

1. After ten minutes, stop and place a star next to those mannerisms and habits that bother you even on *good days*.
2. Compare your list with the lists of others in the class.
3. Discuss tolerance as it relates to your gripe lists.

# Activity 3-5

## Case Study: Getting Ahead While Getting Along

Read the following case study. Then think about the questions that follow. Answer the questions in the spaces provided.

### Case Study

Bonita is president of the student council. Recently, the council sponsored a walkathon for the March of Dimes. Bonita was on vacation with her parents when the council members planned and organized the entire walkathon. When Bonita returned on the day of the walkathon, she immediately took over the responsibility for leading the group. The walkathon was declared a success. The principal of the high school showed how pleased she was by presenting Bonita with a certificate of recognition. Bonita accepted the certificate for herself and then went back to the council members to show it off.

1. Is Bonita correct in assuming that it is her privilege as president of the council to lead the group on the walkathon?

________________________________________

________________________________________

________________________________________

________________________________________

________________________________________

2. Is Bonita doing the right thing in accepting the certificate for herself? Explain your answer.

________________________________________

________________________________________

________________________________________

________________________________________

________________________________________

3. How can Bonita let the rest of the council members be winners too?

________________________________________

________________________________________

________________________________________

________________________________________

________________________________________

Compare your answers to these questions with the answers given by your classmates.

I J K L M N O P

# Activity 3-6

## Flattery

Read the following article by Sydney J. Harris that is reproduced below.[2] Then answer the questions that follow.

### Why Not a Little Flattery?

Mark Twain once confessed that he could live for three weeks on a compliment, and Mark was not an exceptionally vain man. He was just admitting openly what most of us feel privately.

I never had been one of those high-principled persons who object to flattery because it is "insincere." I don't think there is enough flattery in American life, sincere or insincere. The only kind of flattery to which I have a moral objection is the kind in which the flatterer engages because it will "pay" him. This is bootlicking, and no person of sense or sensibility can help but see through it and despise it.

There is another sort of flattery, however, which is extended not because it gives profit to the donor but because it gives pleasure to the recipient. Most of us need this sort of lift from time to time.

### Compliment Their Weaknesses

We need it in the most unexpected areas. Good-looking people usually do not require to be complimented. They are well aware of their looks, and may even be bored with them. What they need, most likely, is a compliment on their brains or clothes, or family.

When most of us pay a compliment, we generally pay it to the person's strongest, most obvious point. But to do the greatest good, a compliment should be directed to the person's weakest point or what he thinks is his weakest point.

Twain could not be elated because somebody came up and told him what a fine writer he was; the whole world accepted that fact. But he was radiant if someone complimented an invention he had helped develop.

### Einstein, the Fiddler

Einstein was a humble man and only shrugged when told how much his genius had revolutionized our ideas of the universe. But a word of flattery about his violin playing (which was mediocre) would bring a sparkle to his eye.

We are a foolish, vain, and doubtful race; even the strongest among us feel weak in some departments. The skillful flatterer is a boon to society, even when he is insincere, so long as his motive is not tainted with self-interest.

1. Do you agree with the last sentence in the article? Why or why not?

______________________________________

______________________________________

______________________________________

2. Now your teacher will tell you the name of a person in the class. Write a nice statement about that person on a separate

[2]Reprinted with permission, Chicago Sun Times, Copyright © 1991

piece of paper. Give the complimentary statement to the teacher. The teacher will give it to the other person. You will also get a complimentary statement from someone.

3. How did you feel about the nice statement written about you? Saying nice things about one another is a good experience, isn't it?

# Chapter 4
# Organizational Effectiveness

KNOWLEDGE: After reading this chapter, you will be able to:

1. Define *organizational effectiveness.*
2. Explain by example what is meant by "Employers are human beings, too."
3. List and describe four ways in which employers may experience success.
4. Describe ways in which employees can help employers to be successful.
5. Define the following terms or concepts:
   a. Competence.
   b. Loyalty.
   c. Trustworthiness.
   d. Honesty.
   e. Responsibleness.
   f. Industriousness.
6. Describe the employer's role in coaching and mentoring.
7. Compare and contrast the three basic management styles: authoritarian, democratic, and laissez-faire.
8. Explain why employers must delegate duties and responsibilities.

ATTITUDES: After reading this chapter, you will:

1. Recognize that, like employees, employers have human needs.
2. Believe that employers should make profits and have a good reputation.
3. Value the idea that employees have a responsibility to help employers increase profits and achieve growth in the business.
4. Desire to develop traits that will help employees to perform well in their jobs.
5. Believe that all management styles can be effective.
6. Recognize the importance of the responsibilities employers must assume.

*Organizational effectiveness* depends on the degree to which you understand the inner workings of your place of employment. Inner workings include knowing why the organization exists, knowing what your employer expects of you, and knowing how to get along with your employer on a daily basis.

In some ways, your employer may be the single most important person at work with whom you must develop a good human relationship. Certainly fellow employees, customers, and others in the work environment are important. But without a good understanding between you and your employer, you may not stay employed long enough to even get to know others on the job.

After studying the previous chapter, you are aware of how important it is for an employee to be able to get along with fellow employees. You learned that many people do not keep their jobs if they are unable to work well with others. In this chapter you will find that it is equally important for employees to work well with their employers or managers. The importance of developing the skill of getting along with one's employer is, of course, obvious. It is the employer who makes decisions on who is hired, who is retained, and who is terminated from employment. If you learn how to develop a good relationship with an employer or manager, you will be able to enjoy a lengthy period of employment.

## UNDERSTANDING AN EMPLOYER

Who is an employer? For the sake of simplicity, in our discussion we will refer

Illus. 4-1. Your employer can help you understand the inner workings of the organization.

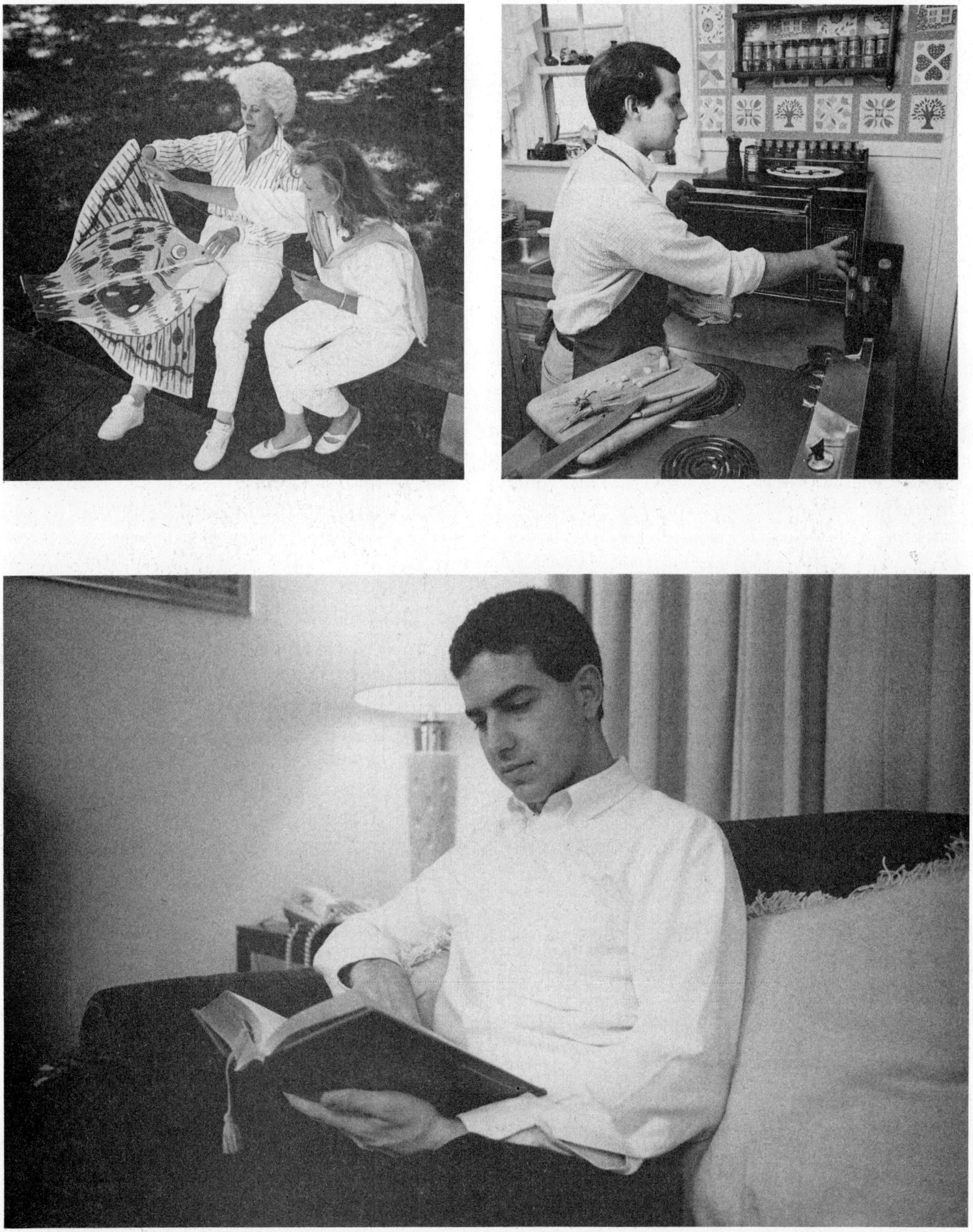

Illus. 4-2. Employers enjoy doing the same things you and I enjoy.

to any person who is in charge of a group of workers as an *employer*. This means that an employer could be the owner of a business or the manager of an organization. Although such persons as department managers, group leaders, floor supervisors, and so on, may not be employers in the strictest sense of the word, they will also be referred to as employers because generally they are in direct charge of a number of employees.

The very nature of an organization demands that someone be in charge and be responsible for its success. This is an inescapable fact. The person in charge has a great deal of responsibility. He or she is usually responsible for such functions as producing goods or services, selling merchandise or services, handling finances, maintaining good housekeeping and safety, purchasing supplies, and many other activities. Your role as an employee is to carry out your employer's suggestions, ideas, and instructions in relation to the responsibilities that your employer holds. Part of carrying out your own responsibilities includes developing the skill with which to complete your assigned duties. An equally important talent is the ability to get along well with your employer. Getting along means working pleasantly with and for your employer for the overall success of the company.

## Employers Are Human Beings, Too

In order to get along with a person and establish a positive relationship, you learned from the previous chapter that it helps to try to understand that person. This is especially true of learning to get along with an employer. Taking a few minutes to think about your employer will pay big dividends in the form of a good working relationship.

Would it surprise you to discover that there are employers who enjoy doing needlepoint, spend every Saturday during the summer at the ball park, ride horses, play pinochle, write poetry, or read books by John Steinbeck? There are also employers who are ham radio enthusiasts, who practice yoga, who cry at weddings, and who have spent two years in fourth grade. You should know and remember that employers and managers are human beings, too. They have good days and bad days just like everyone else. They like to receive compliments and, like the rest of us, sometimes have difficulty accepting criticism. They often forget to give praise and sometimes are too quick to criticize. Many of them probably prefer a vacation over work. And, like employees, they appreciate it when everybody carries his or her own weight. Employers are no different from the rest of us. They have likes and dislikes, wants and needs, pleasures and sorrows, and ups and downs. Learning to accept them as people is the first step toward understanding them.

Looking in on one employer might help you to better understand the human side of employers. Mrs. Christensen is the owner of a large fruit-wholesaling company that supplies retail stores all across the country. She has a large and demanding business and has many employees. As the widowed mother of three children, she is very concerned about their development. She knows it is important to spend a lot of time with her children, and she tries to do that. She has complete responsibility for maintaining a household and small acreage. A painful type of arthritis that flares up for a few days every month is causing her increasing concern. On top of all this, Mrs. Christensen also tries to stay active in her club because she feels it is important for her to remain socially active.

If all of Mrs. Christensen's employees

Illus. 4-3. Mrs. Christensen watches the grading of fruit in her warehouse.

knew and remembered these facts about her, they probably would be better able to relate to her. In developing a good relationship with an employer, it helps to remember that every employer has a human side that is often not visible to the naked eye.

| SUCCESS FORMULA | Sales |
|---|---|
| | Less Costs of Doing Business |
| | Profit |

Illus. 4-4. Making a profit means being successful.

## Success Means Many Things to Employers

An employer may be managing either a profit-making or a nonprofit organization. Nonprofit organizations include institutions engaged in governmental, educational, religious, and charitable activities. In this chapter, however, we are primarily concerned with employers who manage profit-making organizations or businesses. To such employers, success can come in many forms.

### *Making a Profit*

All employers engaged in business want to make a profit. In order to make a profit, businesses must offer goods or services for sale to the public. Making a profit means having extra money left after all of the costs of doing business have been paid. The costs of doing business include such items as the cost of materials used to manufacture goods or the cost of merchandise that is to be sold, wages and salaries paid to employees, interest paid to banks on borrowed funds, supplies, taxes, and other money paid out by the business. All employers engaged in business, therefore, will feel successful if their businesses make a profit.

### *Achieving Growth of the Business*

In addition to profit, many employers work for the growth of their businesses. Growth can mean different things and take many forms. Growth can mean expanding a store by making it larger or building more stores. It can mean increasing the amount of goods or services that a business sells or offers for sale. Growth might also mean hiring additional employees. In many cases, growth cannot take place unless the company is making a profit. Thus, growth and profits usually spell success to most employers.

Brok's Chicken Barbecue chain provides a good example of a business that is both profitable and growing. While still a student, Charlie Brok opened a small chicken barbecue stand next to the university he was attending. He hired other students to work at the stand while he was attending classes or studying. His barbecued chicken was good. And because his employees worked hard and were very cooperative, Charlie's business prospered and grew. Soon he opened a second stand on the other end of the campus. It, too, became successful. After Charlie graduated, he was able to open up two more chicken barbecue stands in other parts of the city. If the present pattern of producing a good product (chicken barbecue) and maintaining good employer-employee relationships continues, the Brok's Chicken Barbecue chain will surely keep on growing.

### *Enjoying a Good Reputation*

Most employers consider themselves successful if they enjoy a respected reputation in their community. A good reputation is one that is earned over a period of years. It is earned by running a company that is honest and ethical. To gain community respect, the company must provide goods or services of high quality and stand behind them. The company must be fair to its employees. It must respect the environment in which it is located. And it should put some of its profits back into the community in the form of charitable contributions.

### *Counting Success in Other Ways*

Other employers might count success in additional ways. To some, a reputation for offering the finest goods or services in an area may be an important factor. To others, success may mean winning a competitive battle with a similar business down the street or across town. To still others, success might appear in the form of receiving awards from the local Chamber of Commerce for having the most satisfied employees.

## WHAT AN EMPLOYER EXPECTS OF EMPLOYEES

An employer expects employees to work together toward achieving the objectives of the company. The wise employee who is interested in having a good relationship with an employer will try to help the employer achieve success.

### Helping to Increase Profits

As an employee you should do everything possible to help increase your em-

Illus. 4-5. An employee filling out an Employee Suggestion Plan form.

ployer's profits. You can do this in several ways. You should give an honest day's work for a day's pay. You should try to save money and time whenever possible. And you can offer suggestions to your employer on ways in which you feel that time and money could be saved.

One well-known United States company has formalized the old concept of a suggestion box into an employee suggestion plan. The plan is called "Everybody's Business" and offers large cash awards for employee suggestions that will help the company reduce costs, increase sales, or improve service.

In this company they say that they need all of the good employee suggestions they can get to help them hold down costs of doing business, to make them more competitive, and to help provide the best service they possibly can. They promise to get employees' suggestions to the right people right away, to evaluate them, and to benefit the entire company if the suggestions are feasible. Any employee is eligible to submit a suggestion and receive a cash award. Through this program and others like it in many companies, employees can contribute to the growth of a business and to excellent human relations between employers and employees.

## Helping to Achieve Growth

As an employee there are many ways you can help your employer's company grow. You can learn to handle more work in the same amount of time. You can tell your friends, relatives, and others about your employer's company and encourage them to patronize it. You can try to think of new products or services that your employer's company could offer. You might think of a location for an additional business for your employer.

Carlos was a sales representative for a firm selling hospitalization insurance. He believed that if he could sell hospitalization insurance to large groups of people, he would be able to make more money, and his company would be able to grow. Carlos signed up for an adult night class in selling group insurance at the local community college. He learned a great deal about the benefits of group insurance plans. He learned that group plans were beneficial both to clients in the form of less expensive premiums and to his company in the form of increased profits. Carlos soon learned enough about group plans to begin selling them.

Carlos experienced much success in selling insurance plans to groups of teachers, labor union members, bankers, city

Illus. 4-6. Carlos attends an evening class.

employees, as well as to many others. His efforts resulted not only in increasing his income, but also in helping his company to grow. This pleased his employer. Carlos' efforts also improved his already good standing with his company.

## Developing Desirable Traits

An employer, in return for salary or wages and fringe benefits paid to employees, expects employees to develop certain desirable traits that will help them to perform their jobs well. Some of these traits include: (1) competence, (2) loyalty, (3) trustworthiness, (4) honesty, (5) responsibleness, and (6) industriousness.

### *Competence*

An employer expects employees to be competent. This means that employees are expected to know what they are supposed to do and how they should perform their jobs. It is assumed, of course, that employees have had training or preparation for the jobs they were hired to perform. Many would-be employees begin to develop competence when they enroll in vocational education classes while still at school. As a rule, competent employees get along well with their employers.

### *Loyalty*

One owner of a company used to say to employees, "If there is something you don't like about our company, please tell us. And if there is something you like about us, please tell others." This employer was really saying that, in return for salary and benefits, the firm expected loyalty from its employees.

Loyalty to a company means going to your supervisor with any problem or complaint that may arise. Part of your supervisor's job is to handle employee problems. Employers prefer to solve their own problems. They do not want dissatisfied employees to complain about their work to outsiders. In the same manner, employers do not want their employees to criticize the goods or services sold by the company to others outside the company.

Loyalty to a company also means telling outsiders about the fine products or services that your company sells. For example, let us take the case of Leslie, a high school student and part-time employee in a bicycle sales and service shop. One of

Illus. 4-7. Leslie is proud of her employer's bicycle products.

the benefits of working for ACE Bicycle Company was the privilege of buying a bicycle for 50 percent off the selling price. After saving enough money, Leslie bought a gleaming ACE ten-speed. It was everything one could want in a new bike. Leslie was very proud of it. She spent a lot of time telling her friends and others what excellent products ACE sold. As a result, many people she knew came into the store and bought bicycles. Of course, this made Leslie's employer very happy.

### *Trustworthiness*

There are many cases when an employer or supervisor is able to place an employee in a position of trust. When an employer trusts an employee, it often means that the employer can ask the employee to do something beyond the call of duty and expect the employee to accomplish it. The special task could be closing up a business at the end of the day. It might involve taking the company car to another city to pick up a business associate. Each of these situations requires that the employer trust the employee to carry out the task. When the employee completes the task, he or she earns the employer's or supervisor's trust. This trust contributes to good human relations between employers and employees.

### *Honesty*

Another trait closely allied to trustworthiness is honesty. This is a trait that gets a lot of attention in many books. Establishing a reputation for honesty is important in developing a good relationship with an employer, especially because one of businesses' greatest problems is dishonest employees.

To be an honest employee means several things. It means, of course, never to take any money or goods that don't belong to you. It means never to say you worked longer than you actually did. It means never to cheat a customer, another employee, or your employer in any way. It can also mean telling your employer and others the truth when you are questioned. If you can prove to be an honest employee, you will be well on your way to acceptability and good human relations in any business.

### *Responsibleness*

Responsibleness is like trustworthiness. A responsible employee is one who agrees to carry out a task under agreed-upon procedures.

Employees are often put in positions where they are responsible for money, for other people's safety, for other people's production, for merchandise, for customers' goodwill, for company equipment, and so on. Employers are quick to see which employees can handle positions and situations of responsibility and which cannot. Needless to say, employers like to have employees who are responsible persons.

Usually employers begin by asking employees to be responsible for less important things. Then they gradually make employees responsible for more important matters. This gradual buildup of responsibility leads to rewards and good relationships between employers and employees.

Let us look at the case of Valery, a new employee of Pete's Flower Shop. Soon after she was hired, Valery was asked to drive the store van to the airport to pick up a small shipment of flowers from Hawaii. She made it to the airport all right. But on the way back to the store, Valery stopped by a friend's house, turned off the van's engine, and talked awhile.

While the engine was stopped, the van's air conditioner was not keeping the flowers cool. They were all ruined from the heat. In this case, Valery did not prove herself to be a responsible employee. Her employer would naturally hesitate to give her a task that involves a greater responsibility in the future.

### *Industriousness*

Industriousness means hard work. It does not necessarily mean physically tiring labor. Rather, industriousness means being diligent about one's duties at work. It is doing what one is paid to do, and possibly more. An industrious person does not loaf, daydream, or otherwise spend large amounts of nonproductive time. Industrious employees try to accomplish their assigned work within the prescribed time. They keep themselves productively occupied during work hours.

It has been said by some people that hard work is its own reward. That is, the satisfied feeling one gets when a good day's work is finished or when a task is completed is a rewarding experience. Furthermore, hard work by an employee is soon rewarded by an employer. Employers are quick to note which of their employees are hardworking and productive and which are "goofing off." The industrious workers are usually rewarded with better pay, promotions, and special privileges.

In summary, when a company hires a person, it expects that person to contribute to the success and growth of the company. Employees can contribute to their employer's success and growth by developing competence, loyalty, trustworthiness, honesty, responsibleness, and industriousness. An employee who posseses these desirable traits will enjoy a very good working relationship with any employer.

## EMPLOYERS MAY BE COACHES AND MENTORS

Your career may be enhanced if your employer becomes your coach and even more so if your employer is your mentor.

Illus. 4-8. Valery was not acting responsibly; all the flowers in the van were wilted.

When your employer or manager serves as your coach, it is like having a private tutor. Coaches help you learn the inner workings of the organization by:

- Providing advice and giving you the benefit of her or his experience.
- Assisting you in making contacts that will help you in your work.
- Directing you to sources of useful information.
- Serving as a sounding board for your ideas and then helping you try out those ideas on others.
- Giving you feedback on your work performance and your interpersonal behavior.

You have the responsibility for establishing the coaching relationship. To do this, you must demonstrate that you are coachable and worth the investment of your employer. The best way to show you are coachable is to develop the traits described earlier in the chapter. You must also initiate coaching sessions with your employer. During these sessions ask for help, advice, information, or feedback. Let your employer know you want his or her guidance. If you sincerely ask for your employer's counsel, you will likely develop your employer into your coach.

A mentor is a special coach who takes a personal interest in your career development. Coaches become mentors for at least three reasons. The first reason is that

Illus. 4-9. Let your employer know you want his or her guidance.

you have demonstrated that your work is better than the work of others in your group or unit. At the same time, you have been able to balance the need for teamwork with your individual success. A second reason is that employers or managers have a duty to find and develop talent and future leaders. A third reason your employer or manager may mentor you is that she or he likes and respects you.

Unfortunately, you have little control over whether someone likes you. You do have a great deal of control over being disliked! When employers like you enough to be your mentor it is probably because you remind them of themselves or of someone in the past that they liked or admired.

The care and development your mentor gives may include:

- Assuring that you have growth opportunities such as working on special projects, task forces, or committees.
- Giving you exposure or visibility to key people in the organization.
- Coaching you on your work and behavior (as described in the section on coaching).
- Sponsoring you for promotions to greater responsibility (and, of course, greater pay).
- Promoting you when the mentor is promoted.

Your responsibilities in establishing a mentoring relationship with an employer or manager are (1) demonstrating you are coachable, (2) showing appreciation for the special opportunities you receive, and (3) working smarter and harder to prove you are worthy of the mentoring efforts of your manager or employer.

## BASIC MANAGEMENT STYLES OF EMPLOYERS

One of an employer's main jobs is to manage people. Managing people means keeping track of and directing the work of employees. Managing people may include determining work hours and planning work schedules. It could include solving problems and giving praise where it is due. Managing people often involves hiring and terminating employees.

There are different ways in which the job of managing employees is carried out. These ways are called *management styles.* An employee who wishes to be effective in the organization should try to identify the employer's management style. Once an employee masters this technique, he or she is well on the way to good relations with the employer and a high degree of organizational effectiveness.

Most management styles are slightly different from one another, and they vary in popularity. However, management styles can usually be classified into three basic categories: (1) authoritarian, (2) democratic, and (3) laissez-faire (pronounced "*lay say fair*"). Each of these basic management styles has its identifying characteristics. See if you can identify any characteristics that will help you to recognize the management style of the three different managers described in the following paragraphs.

### Authoritarian Management Style

Mr. Brandigan is the owner and manager of a service station. He has owned and managed the station for many years. He takes a great deal of pride in referring to the station as "his" business. He started his business all by himself with very little money and a lot of hard work. His business has now increased in size so that he must employ several persons.

Each of Mr. Brandigan's employees reports directly to him. He tells them what hours to work, what clothing to wear, and when they should take their breaks. He instructs them to come to him with all of their questions. Rarely does he ask advice from any of his employees. Mr. Brandigan likes to be in charge of the entire business. His relationship with his employees is definitely that of a leader with a group of followers.

As you may have guessed, Mr. Brandigan displays the characteristics of an *authoritarian leader*. This style of leadership, or management style, allows employees little freedom to think, plan, and make decisions on their own. Some people react negatively to this style, while others like it. Some employees feel that it is easier to work for an authoritarian employer because they want to avoid, whenever possible, the difficult tasks of planning and decision making. Those employees who need a great deal of direction in order to be effective would most likely get along very well with an authoritarian employer.

## Democratic Management Style

Ms. Fernandez owns a company that also employs several people. She holds many meetings during which she seeks the advice and ideas of her employees. For example, Ms. Fernandez allows her employees to help her determine their vacation schedules, sick-leave policies, and parking lot arrangements. She is often gone from the office, leaving others in charge. In general, she encourages them to work together to help her run the company.

It is probably obvious that Ms. Fernandez is a *democratic leader*. An employer who uses the democratic leadership style allows employees to participate in the management of the company by seek-

Illus. 4-10. Mr. Brandigan runs his service station with an authoritarian style of management.

Illus. 4-11. Many employees appreciate an opportunity to become involved in the democratic management of a company.

ing their ideas and suggestions. Thus, this style is also known as *participative management.* It is designed to profit from the ideas of several people. Many employees like this management style because it allows them to feel as though they are really a part of the company. It makes them think that their ideas are worth something. Others dislike this style because they feel that it is clumsy and inefficient. Such employees feel that decision making is the boss's job and that they are just there to work.

Illus. 4-12. When delegating duties, the employer may make one employee responsible for keeping the financial records.

## Laissez-Faire Management Style

Beth and Julius Bergman are licensed interior designers. They own and operate a business that specializes in the interior design of large city apartments. The Bergmans have hired two professional designers to work for them. They assign customers to each of these professional employees and then leave the employees on their own. That is, these professional employees are free to decide how much time to spend with each customer, how many hours they wish to work, which is the best way to work with each customer, and even how much money to charge each customer for services rendered. These professional employees were hired by the Bergmans to do a job. That job is to provide satisfactory interior decorating services. When and how these services are provided is left to the creative imagination and business experience of each employee—each to his or her own style.

As you can see, the Bergmans are *laissez-faire leaders.* Laissez-faire literally means "hands off," and this is the way the Bergmans deal with their employees. Note that the main characteristic of the laissez-faire style of management is employee freedom. Many employees are comfortable with this management style, but some are not. There are employees who become frustrated when faced with this much freedom because they have always had directions given to them and plans made for them. Such employees are afraid that their employer might not like what they create.

To summarize, each of these basic management styles has aspects that some people like and that others dislike. Although at times an employer may use a mixture of management styles, it is important to understand that most employers have management styles that can be readily identified. It is important because, once these styles are understood, the employee who wishes to develop good relations with an employer will learn to deal with the particular management style of that employer. An employee should develop such skills as independence, obedience, and decision making to be able to adapt to different management styles. A good relationship will result when employee skills and management styles are matched.

## WHAT IT'S LIKE TO BE AN EMPLOYER

In your study of human relations, there are two reasons why it might be helpful for you to assume the role of an employer. First, it will help you to understand human relations and management from an employer's point of view. Second, it will be helpful for you to assume the role of an employer because someday you may be an employer or manager yourself.

Pretend for a moment that you are the owner of a business. As the owner or manager you are responsible for many things. You must see to it that the company maintains a reputation for honesty and quality. The company must not only promptly pay all of its debts, but also earn a profit. It needs to remain on good terms with its suppliers. It also needs to remain on good terms with other firms in the community. Accurate financial records must be kept by the company. Also, the company premises must be kept neat and clean, as well as safe, both for customers and employees. These are only some of your many responsibilities.

During a typical day at work you will be the first to arrive, the last to leave, or sometimes both. You will spend a lot of time talking on the telephone and meeting with employees and customers. You will have very little time for yourself. You will also have little time to think over a decision. Most of your decisions will deal with who does what, how much time is given to get something done, and how much money will be spent on equipment or supplies. At any moment you will be expected to referee disagreements between employees or with customers. You must show a personal interest in each employee, but stop short of getting involved in his or her personal life.

The ultimate responsibility for successfully running an organization rests with its owner or manager. This person must see to it that everything and everybody in the organization works, and works together. To carry responsibility for all the duties involved in running an organization is usually too much for one person alone. This is why a *delegation* of duties takes place. This means that the employer or manager assigns certain responsibilities and duties to various employees. The larger the organization, the more duties are delegated.

For example, the employer may make one employee responsible for keeping the financial records. Another employee may be made responsible for keeping the premises clean. Still another might be made responsible for maintaining good relationships with other firms in the community. But the responsibility of getting along with one another lies with each and every employee.

An employer, therefore, is most pleased when all the employees carry out the responsibilities given them. Now that you have a fairly good idea of what it's like to be an employer, you should try your best to carry out all responsibilities given to you and work hard to maintain good relations with your employer.

# Activity 4-1

## Who Is an Employer?

You know that an employer is any person in an organization who is in charge of a group of workers. In the spaces provided below, list as many employers as you can think of who live in your community. Then compare your list with the lists of others in your class. Did any of you name some of the same employers?

| Name of Employer | Name of Organization |
|---|---|
| | |
| | |
| | |
| | |
| | |
| | |
| | |
| | |
| | |
| | |
| | |

# Activity 4-2

## Interviewing an Employer

Yes, employers are human. This activity will provide an opportunity for you to find out firsthand. You should arrange to interview an employer in your community (perhaps one you listed in Activity 4-1). This interview will help you get to know an employer and will get you started toward good relations with employers.

To help you with the interview, a list of questions you might ask the employer is given below. In the spaces provided, jot down the answers given to you during the interview.

1. How long have you been an employer?

_______________________________________

2. How many employees do you supervise?

_______________________________________

3. Do you like your job? Why?

_______________________________________

_______________________________________

_______________________________________

_______________________________________

_______________________________________

4. Does your work sometimes make you irritable or upset? When does this happen?

_______________________________________

_______________________________________

_______________________________________

_______________________________________

_______________________________________

5. What kind of employee do you get along with best?

_______________________________________

_______________________________________

_______________________________________

_______________________________________

_______________________________________

6. Do you have a mentor? Are you mentoring someone? Why or why not?

_______________________________________

_______________________________________

_______________________________________

_______________________________________

_______________________________________

7. What is the best part of your job? Why is it the best part?

_______________________________________

_______________________________________

_______________________________________

_______________________________________

_______________________________________

# Activity 4-3

## The Employee Suggestion Plan

This activity will give you some experience in providing a positive suggestion to an organization. Assume that your classroom is a business and your teacher is your employer. Please fill in the blanks on the Employee Suggestion Plan (Illus. 4-12) with a positive suggestion that will improve your employer's business or work activities. Perhaps your teacher will have a reward for the best suggestion.

Mountain Bell

8750
(1-84)

**EVERYBODY'S BUSINESS** Employee Suggestion Plan

| FOR OFFICE USE ONLY | | | |
|---|---|---|---|
| Date Received | Suggestion Number | Segment Coordinator | |

**HOW TO MAKE SUGGESTIONS** 1. Read the General Rules of the Suggestion Plan (back of form). 2. Tell exactly what your idea is. Suggest ideas that have one or more of these results: • Improves customer service • Increases revenues • Decreases expense • Reduces capital requirements • Improves operating efficiency • Improves safety • Improves security • Contributes significantly toward Company goals. Suggestions not eligible for award consideration include, among others: • Matters covered by collective bargaining (Labor Contract) • Suggestions which fail to define a problem and/or solution • Slogans of any type • Conditions that could or should be corrected through normal maintenance or supervisory action • Suggestions producing only personal benefit to the suggester • Matters already under consideration due to previous suggestions or regular management function • Suggestions that would involve the Company in violating legal obligations. 3. Use a separate form for each suggestion. Please be complete; attach additional sheets if necessary. 4. Explain, in detail, how your idea could be implemented. 5. Illustrate your idea if appropriate (Often a sketch or model is needed to back up your written description, particularly on form changes and redesign of equipment. Also, a sample of the item under discussion helps). 6. Be neat. Several people must read your idea.

**PLEASE TYPE OR PRINT NEATLY, PRESS FIRMLY - YOU ARE MAKING FOUR COPIES!**

Here is the problem/condition needing improvement: ____________

Here is what should be done: ____________

Here is how the company will benefit: ____________

Check as appropriate:

☐ Extra sheets attached ☐ Form and/or sketch enclosed ☐ Model sent

**FILL IN EACH BLANK COMPLETELY AND ACCURATELY**

| First Name | Last Name | Segment | Social Security Number | Payroll Number |
|---|---|---|---|---|

| Work Address | Street | Room | City | State | Zip Code | Work Telephone Number |
|---|---|---|---|---|---|---|
| Home Address | Street | Apt. | City | State | Zip Code | Home Telephone Number |

Send Correspondence To: ☐ Work ☐ Home

☐ Mgt. ☐ Non Mgt.

Mgt. Level ____________

Title ____________

Date | Signature

This suggestion is submitted for consideration under the terms and conditions of the Mountain Bell Employee Suggestion Plan as explained on the back of this form and in I.M. 197.

**USE COMPANY INTER-OFFICE MAIL ENVELOPES WHEN POSSIBLE TO REDUCE MAILING COSTS.**

Mail To: **EVERYBODY'S BUSINESS**
930 - 15th Street Rm. 540
Denver, Colorado 80202

**SUGGESTION PLAN OFFICE FILE COPY**

Illus. 4-13. Employee suggestion plan.

# Activity 4-4

## Dealing with Authoritarian, Democratic, and Laissez-Faire Employers

You have read about three leadership or management styles an employer may adopt. After reading the situations given in Illus. 4-14, write in the blank spaces how you think an employer with each style would react to each situation.

| Situation | AUTHORITARIAN | DEMOCRATIC | LAISSEZ-FAIRE |
|---|---|---|---|
| You are a salesperson and an irate customer continues to harass you weekly about the low quality of the goods the store sells. | | | |
| You are a hospital admissions clerk and a person comes to your desk wishing to solicit contributions for a charity from the nurses and physicians. | | | |
| You and one other employee want a cold-drinks machine installed in the employees' lounge. | | | |

Illus. 4-14. Different management styles.

# Activity 4-5

## What Leadership Style Would You Choose?

Assume that you are the owner of a small convenience food store. At the bottom of this page, tell which management style you would adopt (authoritarian, democratic, or laissez-faire) and why you would adopt that particular style. Then discuss your writings in class.

# Activity 4-6

## Identifying Authoritarian, Democratic, and Laissez-Faire Leaders

In the blank before each of the statements listed below, place an *A*, *D*, or *L*, depending on whether you think the statement describes an authoritarian, democratic, or laissez-faire leader. Discuss your answers with other students in the class.

1. ___ Wants all concerns to be brought to the employer's attention.
2. ___ Encourages votes by the employees in meetings.
3. ___ Wants employees to solve their own problems.
4. ___ Is usually a very strong leader.
5. ___ Asks advice of employees.
6. ___ Encourages independent work.
7. ___ Hires people to do a job in the way best suited to them.
8. ___ Feels group decisions are the best.

Chapter 5
# Customer Focus

**KNOWLEDGE:** After reading this chapter, you will be able to:

1. Define the term *customer*.
2. Describe why customers return to a business to buy more goods or services.
3. Define in three different ways what *goodwill* means.
4. Describe ways to recognize customers and remember their names.
5. State some guidelines for dealing with customers.
6. State the meaning of the phrase, "The customer is always right."
7. Analyze the statement, "It's business, not personal."

ATTITUDES: After reading this chapter, you will:

1. Recognize the importance of retaining customers.
2. Believe goodwill helps businesses to attract and keep customers.
3. Recognize the value of remembering customers' names and details about them.
4. Accept the practical view of the concept, "The customer is always right."
5. Accept customers' feelings without arguing.
6. Be able to view a transaction through the eyes of a customer

It has been repeated often that the most important component of any business is its customers. Getting along with customers is important for all those associated with a business. Learning to know, understand, and relate to customers in any business is a skill that will give multiple rewards.

## WHO IS A CUSTOMER?

Most businesses, as you have learned before, exist to make a profit. That is, they either take or create a good or service, add some value to it, and then sell it for more money than they paid for it. The persons to whom businesses sell their goods or services are generally called customers.

The term *customer* can be applied to different kinds of persons. A customer could be a child buying a toy, a parent buying a life insurance policy, or a purchasing agent buying a bus for a city. A customer might be a person buying a theater ticket, a man getting a haircut, or a woman buying a tennis racket. A *customer* is anyone who has a need and who can buy something from a business to fill that need.

## THE IMPORTANCE OF CUSTOMERS

You probably already have a fairly good idea of why customers are important to businesses. It has been said that "nothing happens in business until somebody buys something." Without customers, businesses couldn't exist. Customers buy the goods and/or services that businesses offer to the public. Companies must pay the expenses of doing business with the money that the customers spend. In most cases, there will be some money left over after the company pays the costs of doing business. The money left over becomes the profit of the business. What the quote really means, then, is that no business can succeed unless it earns a profit.

Thus, you can see that the most important element in a business is its customers because they are the ones who contribute to profits. It literally pays to learn to get along with customers. For if you do, your customers will return time and again to your business and continue to buy goods or services.

## WHY CUSTOMERS KEEP COMING BACK

There are three main reasons why customers patronize, or keep coming back to, any particular business. These are: (1) good-quality products, (2) good-quality service, and (3) goodwill. Most customers take their business to specific establishments for one or any combination of these reasons.

### Good-Quality Products

The first reason why customers keep coming back to a business is good products. No store, factory, wholesale warehouse, or mail-order company will stay in business long if it produces and/or sells inferior products. The goods that a business sells to its customers must be of high and lasting quality. The goods must do what the seller says they will do. The goods must be safe and clean. The reputations of some businesses have suffered because they have offered goods of less than top quality to customers. When this happens, customers are disillusioned and buy

Illus. 5-1. There are many varieties of customers.

elsewhere. Employees in businesses should work to see that this doesn't happen. Above all, a customer must be satisfied with the product(s).

## Good-Quality Services

Some businesses sell only services. Such businesses deal in *intangibles,* or things that you can't actually touch or keep in your possession as you would, for example, a pair of shoes. Examples of companies that sell services are those that provide entertainment such as the theater, the bowling alley, and the ball park; those that sell insurance policies to protect people against loss or damage to automobiles or homes; and those that extend credit such as banks that loan money to people and charge interest for the use of that money.

Other businesses provide services to accompany the products that they sell. For example, automobile dealerships repair cars that they sell; television stores repair and adjust television sets that they sell; businesses that sell sewing machines often give lessons on how to operate the machines; furniture stores usually deliver furniture; and air conditioning dealers also install the units in people's homes.

The various services that businesses sell must be of high quality, legal, and fairly priced, and they must provide satisfaction or pleasure. The service must be safe, and it must be provided without discrimination to all who want to buy it.

## Goodwill

Most businesses can sell good-quality products, and many of them are able to provide satisfactory services. Whether a

Illus. 5-2. Customers come to a business expecting good products, good service, and goodwill.

Illus. 5-3. These businesses sell good-quality products.

business sells goods or services, there is another commodity it must also offer if it wants customers to keep coming back. This commodity is an intangible item called goodwill.

## *Various Forms of Goodwill*

Goodwill has several definitions and can mean different things to different people. In general, however, it might be said that *goodwill* is the friendly, honest, generous, courteous, and kind feeling that a company might project and that a customer might expect.

***Good Reputation.*** One form of goodwill has already been hinted at earlier in this chapter. It is the good reputation that accompanies the offer of high-quality goods and services. Customers usually feel very good about a company when they know that they have received their

Illus. 5-4. These businesses sell good-quality services.

"money's worth." No amount of any other kind of goodwill can substitute for high-quality merchandise and excellent services.

***Generosity.*** Goodwill may also be dispensed in the form of generosity. For example, stores may give away toys to children, offer free gift-wrapping, or provide carry-out or delivery services. Some companies give coupons for free goods or services, provide free alterations, or give away specialty advertising items such as pencils, calendars, or balloons. Most customers readily accept and appreciate this type of goodwill.

***Attitude toward Customers.*** Perhaps the most important and meaningful variety of goodwill that can be offered comes from the people working for the company. That is, the source of this goodwill is the employees and the employers, *not* give-away items. This type of goodwill is the best because it is remembered longest by customers and because it costs nothing to give. It is a genuine helpful attitude, it is a friendly manner, and it is a pleasant smile. It is remembering and recognizing customers, and knowing their likes, dislikes, and sizes. Customer goodwill also means always showing courtesy and understanding. It is being respectful of privacy and not being pushy or overbearing. Being a pleasant and considerate person will almost automatically result in improved customer

Illus. 5-5. Goodwill may be dispensed in the form of free delivery.

relations and greater overall goodwill for a business.

When customers enter a business—whether it is a hotel, a TV repair shop, or a manufacturing plant—they are usually there because they have a need. Customers expect to pay money for what they want. And in exchange for that money, they want a product or service and someone pleasant to help them obtain the exact product or service they desire.

### *Recognizing Customers and Remembering Their Names*

Almost everyone likes to be recognized. We like it when people remember our names, our hobbies, our birthdays, or something else about us. Customers are no exception. They, too, appreciate recognition. It gives them a certain feeling of importance. People will naturally return as customers to businesses where they are recognized and made to feel welcome. This is a very important fact to understand and to put into practice for anyone who owns or works in a business.

A popular way to give recognition to customers is simply to remember their names and use those names when greeting them. Try to think back to a time when an employee in a store or other organization greeted you by name. That probably made you feel recognized and accepted. In a small- or medium-size organization, this is not too difficult to accomplish. In a large organization that serves thousands of people, it can be quite a hard task. It is true that remembering names can be hard. But a few hints will help you to remember many names of customers even in a large organization.

***Watch for a Person's Name.*** The first hint is to watch for a person's name. Customers' names will appear on credit cards, drivers' licenses, bank checks, business cards, name tags, desk signs, office doors, uniforms or clothing, or in a dozen other places. The trick, then, is to use the name in a greeting ("Hi, Ms. Perez"), in a farewell ("Thanks for stopping at the shop, Frank"), or in a conversation ("This jacket should last for several years, Mrs. Taylor"). Repeating names will help you to remember them.

***Work Out Word Associations.*** Another way to help you remember names is to work out word associations. That is, take a person's name and try (privately) to associate it with some unique characteristic of that person. For example, assume that the person's name is Ms. Brownlee and she has long, brown hair. In this case it should be rather easy to remember that the woman with long, brown hair is named Ms. Brownlee. But do be careful to observe when she cuts or tints her hair! You could have fun developing different word associations for people you know and meet.

***Develop a Card File of Customers.*** Still another way to help you remember customers' names is to start a card file. This is simply a file of 3" × 5" cards that contain the customers' names. Looking through this file during your free hours will help you to remember names.

The card file may also contain other useful information about your customers. For example, if you are a salesperson in a clothing store, your card file would contain each customer's size, favorite colors, taste in fashion, and perhaps even age or occupation. An automobile dealer's customer card file would contain information about customers' cars such as age, model, and make.

It is probably obvious that a card file of customers could serve at least two purposes. First, the file will help you remember details about a customer that will help you recognize that customer. In addition to their names, sizes, and brand preferences, customers also appreciate it when you remember the names of their spouses, parents, or children.

The second purpose of a card file is to help the salesperson sell more goods and services. It is possible to cite several examples of how this purpose can be accomplished. For instance, an employee in a men's clothing store might keep a record of a customer's purchase of new dress suits. After consulting the card file, the employee might find that this customer is six months past his usual date for buying a new suit. The next step for the employee would be to telephone the customer or send him a card, reminding him of some new style or color in a suit that he may prefer. Inviting the customer to come into the store may be just the clincher that will convince him to buy a new suit. When instances like this occur, everyone concerned—the customer, the employer, and the employee—will enjoy goodwill and improved human relations with one another.

Let us take another example. Elaine was a new-car salesperson who kept a file on former customers. She did this as a service to her customers and as a source of potential sales for her. During slow days, Elaine made it a habit to call former

Illus. 5-6. People usually like to be recognized.

customers. She would remind them of needed oil changes or of new products that might improve the performance of their cars. Finally, she would ask them if they might like to stop in and look at a new model.

One day Elaine got Mr. Barlow, a former customer, on the line. As Elaine began describing an economy model that she thought might interest him, he responded by saying that he had just been discussing with his wife the possible purchase of a new car. Elaine convinced Mr. Barlow to come and look at the car. Sure enough, Elaine's card file system paid off when she sold the car to Mr. Barlow.

In summary, goodwill is not only important to getting along with individual customers. Goodwill is valuable because of the role that it plays in the reputation of the business and in the way this reputation is passed on. The reputation of a company is based at least as much on the courtesy, thoughtfulness, kindness, and competence of the people operating the company as it is based on the quality of goods or services that the company sells. People remember when they are treated well. They not only remember, but they also tell others about it. This act of passing the word along is often referred to as *word-of-mouth advertising*. Most companies realize that this is a very valuable type of advertising because it is free and it is thought to have much credibility or truthfulness. Untold numbers of customers patronize a business because a friend or a relative referred to it as a good place to do business. Establishing a good reputation and goodwill with customers will surely make them keep coming back.

## HOW TO DEAL WITH ANY CUSTOMER

Much could be written about how to deal with all of the different types of customers. Customers may be rich or poor, frugal or spendthrift, young or old. They may be grouchy or happy, bright or confused, set in their ways or willing to try anything new. Or customers may be "just looking." It would be a hopeless task to try to develop a set of guidelines on how to get along and improve your relationships with the many categories of customers that exist. It would probably be more useful to develop one set of guidelines that would be appropriate for dealing with *any* customer.

As a background for developing guidelines, it would be proper at this point to review what a customer, or a potential customer, is. We have said that a customer is any person who has a need and who can buy something to fill that need. This definition covers a great number of people. A customer may be one who needs new shoes, change for a parking meter, a used bicycle, or a pair of pliers. Or a customer may be one who is seeking a friendly face, a gift for a grandchild, shelter from the rain, a hot dog, or a fluted gizmo. The point to be emphasized here is that customers have many varying

*Location courtesy of Northland Volkswagen.*

Illus. 5-7. Elaine shows a new car to Mr. Barlow.

characteristics and many different needs. It would be almost impossible to learn to deal individually with too many combinations of characteristics and needs of customers.

## Two Simple Guidelines

The two most important guidelines for dealing with any type of customer are:

1. Learn the customer's need.
2. Try to satisfy the customer's need.

If you remember and practice these guidelines, they will assist you in any kind of situation. To practice these guidelines, however, you will have to adopt a very sensitive and inquisitive style. Furthermore, you will have to work at figuring ways to give the customer what he or she really wants. The best way to introduce you to the skill of practicing these guidelines is to provide examples of people who use them.

## Practicing the Guidelines

Let us take the case of Francisco, an employee in the hardware department of a discount store. He had full responsibil-

Illus. 5-8. Customers have many different needs.

ity for ordering, stocking, displaying, and selling a full line of hardware in his department. One day, while Francisco was hard at work arranging merchandise, an elderly man walked slowly into the hardware department. Francisco said nothing because his was a self-service department where customers were allowed and encouraged to select the merchandise they wanted to buy. Soon the man, who was looking over several items, asked, "Don't you have any six-inch brass hinges?"

"No," replied Francisco, "we only carry four-inch, brass-plated hinges. But three of them are strong enough for most residential uses."

"I didn't think you'd have them," continued the elderly man. "I haven't seen them in years. I once was a carpenter, and that's the only thing we ever used to hang a door."

"That's interesting," said Francisco. "My father is a carpenter, and I think he uses four-inch hinges all the time. They seem to work all right."

"Oh, yes, they work all right," the man said. "But the bigger brass ones are stronger."

"Are you hanging a door?" asked Francisco.

"No," replied the elderly man. "I was just browsing and thought I'd see if anybody still carried any of the big, old brass hinges. Why, I remember one time. . . ."

It is probably obvious to you, just as it was to Francisco, that the elderly man needed someone with whom he could talk. He probably wasn't interested in buying anything. However, there was a chance that, during his browsing, he might have noticed something he needed and bought it. Francisco did a very good job of listening and analyzing the man's need for companionship. He then tried to satisfy the man's need by briefly talking with him and being friendly toward him. By following the guidelines for dealing with any type of customer, Francisco improved his human relations with this potential customer by finding out what the man's needs were and then trying to satisfy them. The elderly man left Francisco's hardware department feeling good. He will probably return one day and buy something from Francisco.

Another example of a person who adopted the two guidelines on dealing with any type of customer was Erin. She was the manager of a small dress shop. One day, as she was taking inventory of some dresses, a customer shyly entered the shop. She looked around nervously and then began to turn toward the door. In a very pleasant voice, Erin said, "How are you today?" Erin asked her if there was anything she could do for her. The customer replied, "Well, I don't know. I was sort of wondering if you might be able to help me select a birthday present for my sister."

Erin said, "Why, certainly. Tell me what you can about her size."

"Hmm, I don't know," the customer said.

"How tall is she?" Erin asked.

"She's about 5 feet 4 inches tall. She weighs about 115 pounds, and I think her waist is about 28 inches."

Illus. 5-9. Francisco attends to a customer who is just browsing.

Illus. 5-10. Erin is good at learning a customer's needs and trying to satisfy them.

"Now, that gives us something to go on," said Erin. "Don't worry, I'll bet we can find a gift she'll really like."

Erin then went on to pick out several dresses from which the customer chose one. She purchased it and left the shop confident and happy. Like Francisco, Erin worked at learning customers' needs and trying to satisfy them. The customer was clearly nervous and uncertain when she entered Erin's shop. Her first need was to be reassured, and her second need was to purchase a gift. Erin did a very good job in this case.

With a little thought and sensitivity and a thorough knowledge of the goods and/or services that your employer provides, you, too, can learn to satisfy customers' needs. The trick is *not* to make assumptions about people and *not* to fall into the bad habit of treating all customers the same way. Rather, the successful employee recognizes that every customer is different and has various needs. Then that employee works to satisfy those needs.

## IS THE CUSTOMER ALWAYS RIGHT?

You have no doubt heard of the phrase, "The customer is always right." Yet you know that it is not possible for anyone to be right *all* of the time. Have you ever wondered what this phrase really means?

The idea that the customer is always right is designed to reflect an *attitude.* That attitude is a good and positive feeling directed toward the customer. It means that the customer's point of view should always be taken into consideration. It also means that an employee should never argue with a customer. Rather, an employee should try very hard to see the customer's viewpoint when working to learn his or her needs.

To illustrate this attitude, take the case of the interaction between Sonja, a service station employee, and one of her customers, Erik. He pulled into the station one day and asked her to fill his car with premium gasoline and to check the engine oil. Sonja had just changed the oil and lubricated Erik's car a week ago. She was certain that the oil could not be low so soon. But, rather than argue with Erik, she quickly checked the oil level and found it to be ok.

Even though Sonja knew she was right, she was wise not to argue with Erik. Arguing would have accomplished nothing. In fact, it could have caused Erik to develop bad feelings toward Sonja and the service station. Then, Erik might have decided to do no more business at that station. By not arguing with Erik, no harm was done. And Erik left with his car full of gas, pleased and feeling that he had received value for his money.

## "IT'S BUSINESS, NOT PERSONAL"

Like the phrase, "The customer is always right," you may have heard the phrase, "It's business, not personal." While the original meaning of this second phrase may refer to a different matter, as an employee you should take comfort in it. Remembering this phrase should make you feel better whenever you are verbally attacked by a customer. (This won't happen often, but it may occur; when it does, it will be helpful to you if you understand what is happening.) Understanding situations like this will help to make you a better employee by improving your human relations with customers.

### Don't Take the Customer's Aggression Personally

Sometimes a customer enters a store looking very upset. Perhaps that customer is taking back a piece of merchandise that has not proved to be satisfactory. Such a customer may have the feeling that he or she has been cheated in some way by not having received his or her "money's worth." In an effort to get a "fair shake," the customer may use aggression. This means that he or she will appear very angry and demand a refund. The customer may also make threatening, accusing, and downgrading statements about the business. Sometimes the customer's statements are directed not only at the business, but also at you, the employee.

Here is where you need to understand that the customer is not really angry at you. Rather, the customer sees aggression as the best way to get what he or she wants. As an employee, you should try not to take the customer's aggression personally. Instead, you should understand it for what it is and go about, as usual, trying to learn the customer's need and to satisfy it. Most often the need will be for you to accept the merchandise being returned and either supply substitute goods or return the customer's money.

Illus. 5-11. Some customers may become very irate.

### Don't Continue the Customer's Argument

One beneficial way to deal with an irate customer is to allow this person to "vent steam" rather than try to "shut it off." You might say, "You seem angry. Let's go back to the break room, and you tell me what your problem is." When the customer feels that you understand and care about his or her feelings, usually the customer will be more ready to calm down and deal with the problem in a reasonable way.

Employees are often tempted to defend themselves against angry customers by saying, "It's not my fault that the handle broke." Although this may be true, it is really continuing an argument that the customer may be trying to start. Often a good solution is simply to accept the customer's feelings by putting yourself in his or her place.

In summary, getting along with customers is a skill that is not difficult to learn. Treating each one of them as you would like to be treated, trying to learn their needs, and trying to satisfy those needs will make you a good employee in any business.

## Activity 5-1

### When Are You a Customer?

Most of us are customers every day. We are customers in many ways. We may buy bus tickets, lunches, movie tickets, records, or sporting goods. We may put money in vending machines or use it to buy postage stamps. You are a customer when you have a need and then buy something to fill that need. More simply, you are a customer whenever you spend money.

You have probably spent some money recently. Try to remember the ways in which you have been a customer by listing the *goods* or *services* you have purchased in the last *two* days. Then compare your list with the lists of others in your class. Did you forget to list something?

# Activity 5-2

## What Happens in Business?

It has been said that "nothing happens in business until somebody buys something." In the space below, tell what you think this phrase means. Then compare your answer with the answers of others in your class.

# Activity 5-3

## Who Are They?

You learned in Chapter 5 that it is important to remember the names of customers. You have also been given hints on how to remember names. Below are photographs of six faces with names printed beneath them. In two minutes try to memorize the names of each of these faces. Then turn the page and, without peeking, write as many names as you can remember.

Erik Elridge

Sandra Hahn

Steve Chang

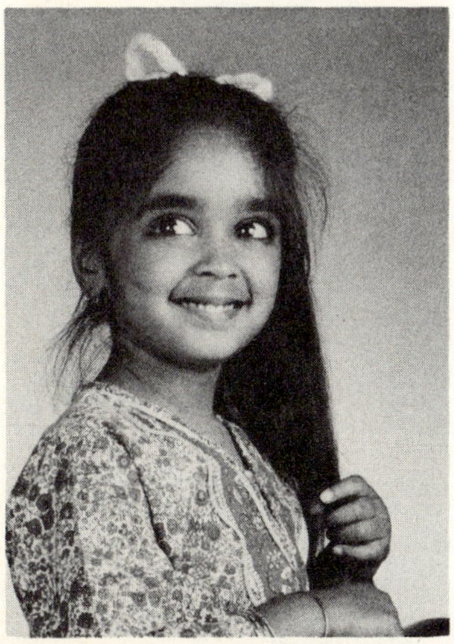

Anu Davidson

John Adams

Helen Johnson

Illus. 5-12. Remembering faces and names.

# Activity 5-4

## The Card File

Below is a customer card from a card file in an appliance store. Study the card, and then make a list of the points you would make in a telephone call to Ms. Arbuckle.

Remember the guidelines for dealing with customers are:

1. Learn the customer's need.
2. Try to satisfy the customer's need.

What points would you make in a telephone call to Ms. Arbuckle?

______________________________

______________________________

______________________________

______________________________

Name: Ms. Ardis Arbuckle

Address: 2121 Vine Street, Lincoln, NE 68508

Telephone: 488-6869

Occupation: University Professor

| Appliances Owned | Date Purchased |
|---|---|
| 12A Refrigerator with Icemaker | 1992 |
| 14B Countertop Microwave Oven | 1990 |
| 10X Washer-Dryer Combo | 1987 |
| 18T Video Cassette Recorder | 1986 |
| 13Y 4-Cycle Dishwasher (Portable) | 1982 |

## Activity 5-5

### Is the Customer Always Right?

For this activity you will have to identify two businesses (preferably one that sells goods and one that sells services). It will be your task to select an owner-manager or assistant manager and ask that person, "What do you think the phrase 'The customer is always right' really means?" Please record a summary of the managers' responses in the spaces below and be prepared to share them with the class.

#### Businessperson 1

#### Businessperson 2

# Chapter 6
# Interpersonal Communication

KNOWLEDGE: After reading this chapter, you will be able to:

1. Define *communication* and draw a model of the communication process.
2. Analyze the statement, "Meanings are in people, not in words."
3. Define and give examples of the problem of semantics.
4. Define *allness* and apply the definition to communication in everyday life situations.
5. Describe the misuse of language by giving examples of labeling, emotional confusion, and sexist language.
6. Apply the following three reasons why people are poor listeners to listening situations in the business world:
   a. People think faster than they speak.
   b. Emotions block out certain messages.
   c. Planning a reply gets in the way of listening.
7. Explain the meaning of "Listen for facts and feelings."
8. List three or more ways to improve listening.
9. Draw formal and informal communication systems, using principles of the formal organization chart.
10. Describe the relationships of the rumor formula to accuracy of the grapevine.

ATTITUDES: After reading this chapter, you will:

1. Believe that meanings are in people, not in words.
2. Recognize the damage to human relations caused by allness.
3. Be concerned about the negative aspects of labeling and emotionally loaded words, as well as sexist language.
4. Enjoy listening for facts and feelings in a message.
5. Gain satisfaction from improving listening.
6. Accept the limitations of the grapevine communication system.
7. Value the use of formal communication in organizations.

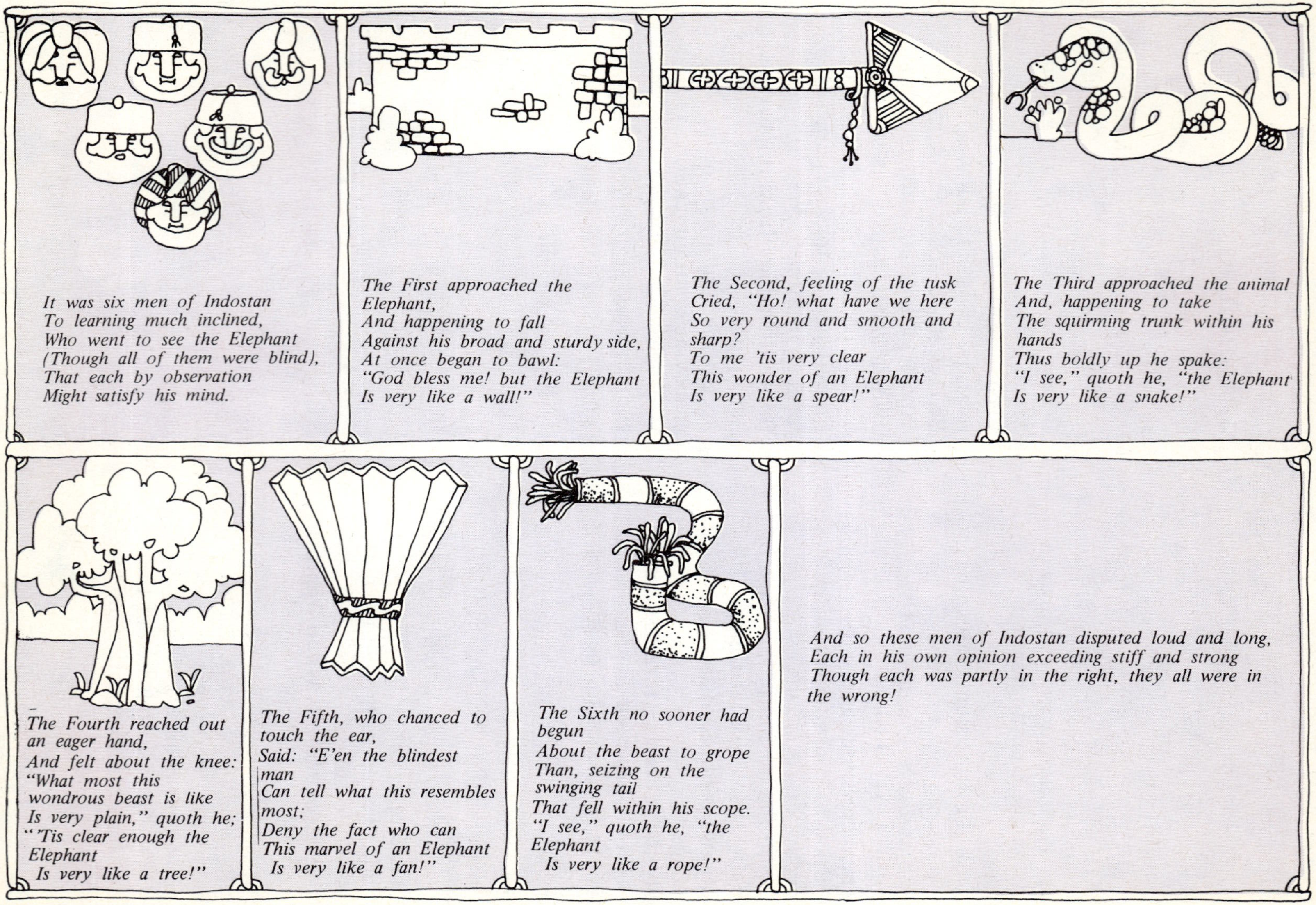


Illus. 6-1. The parable of the blind men and the elephant.

This year employers will spend millions of dollars trying to improve communication. Similar amounts were invested last year, and even more money will be spent next year. Employers will spend thousands of hours attending communication-training programs. Also, thousands of hours will be devoted to communication training for employees. By spending so much time and money on improving communication, one would think that communication problems were under control. The opposite is true. Communication problems are far from being under control.

All of this time and money, however, has not been wasted. Many organizations now have colorful company magazines, eye-catching newsletters, and well-written office memos. Some companies even send birthday cards to their employees. Unfortunately, these kinds of efforts have little effect on improving communication. Why? Because the main problems center on the failure of people to recognize that communication problems are human problems. Emotions, attitudes, and feelings are involved whenever people communicate. The barriers to good communication are a result of human problems.

## DEFINITION OF *COMMUNICATION*

Most managers cannot define good communication. In a recent survey, managers were asked, "What is good communication?" They gave answers such as:

1. Good communication . . . is when workers have good attitudes.
2. Good communication . . . happens when employee turnover is low.
3. Good communication . . . eliminates misunderstandings.

As you can see, the managers responded by describing the *results* of good communication. They were not able to tell what it is, even though they knew when good communication occurred. Defining something by describing only a part of it is not a good method. Consider the parable of the blind men and the elephant in Illus. 6-1. This parable demonstrates the drawback of giving incomplete, or partial, definitions. Each of the blind men described only a small part of the whole elephant. Because each blind man could only describe what one part was like, their individual descriptions of an elephant were surprisingly different from one another, as shown in Illus. 6-2.

How, then, can managers improve something they cannot define? The answer would seem to be this: only with a lot of luck. As a wise student of good human relations and communication in business, you would not wish to depend on plain luck, would you?

*Communication* is a process. The process, shown in Illus. 6-3, is a series of four operations. Here is how it works:

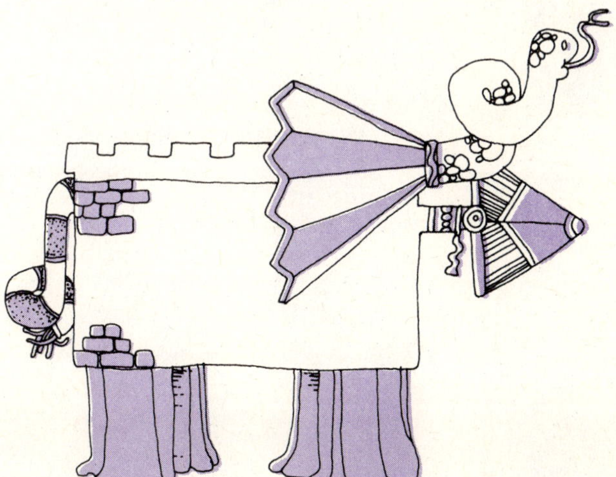

Illus. 6-2. The blind men's individual descriptions of the elephant.

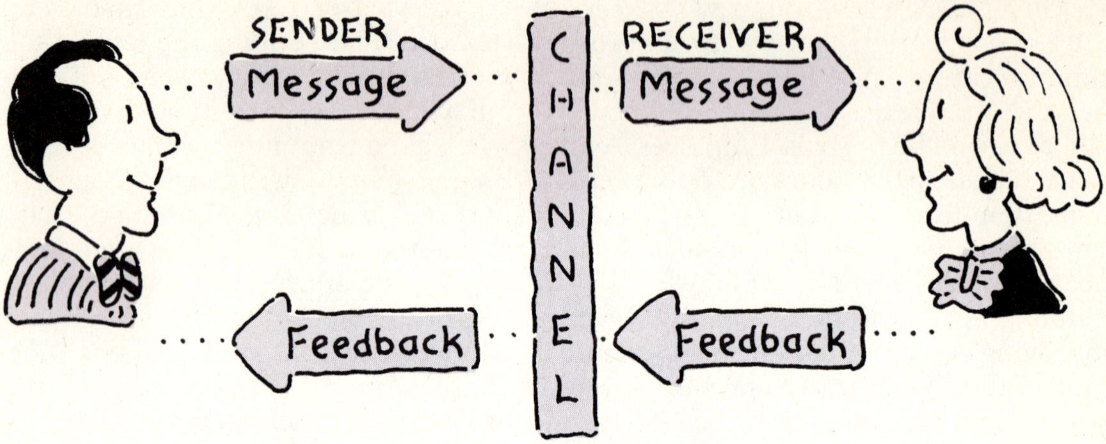


Illus. 6-3. Communication process.

1. A person called the *sender* wants to say something. That something is called a *message*.
2. The Sender then decides how the Message will be sent. In most communication models, this is referred to as *channel selection*. Examples of *channels* include the following:

Oral

- face to face
- small group meeting
- large group meeting

Written

- notes and letters
- memos and reports
- teletype

Sign Language

High Technology

- electronic mail
- videotape, disk
- records and laser disk
- fax

Mass Media

- radio
- television
- newspaper, magazine

Special Signals

- Morse code
- flashing lights
- signaling flags
- smoke signals
- drums

3. A person called the *Receiver* hears the message and decides on a response. The response is called a *feedback*.
4. The Receiver then chooses how the feedback will be sent. Again, there is channel selection for the feedback.

All two-way communication follows the process shown in Illus. 6-3. If the communication is one way, the feedback parts of the process are not used. The process itself always works. Problems develop because people, knowingly or unknowingly, present barriers to the message and the feedback reception.

## BARRIERS TO GOOD COMMUNICATION AND HUMAN RELATIONS

Do you think that words, by themselves, mean the same thing to everyone? If you do, you are like most people who have not studied communication problems. To illustrate this point, answer the following question:

What is the definition of the word *lead*?

The word *lead*, for example, has more than 80 different meanings! What is more, the 500 most common words in the English language have more than 14,000 different meanings. Now you can see why meanings are in people, not in words. Only people can give meaning to words. When a person uses a word, that word is used with just one meaning. The particular meaning is what that person intends the word to mean. Many people overlook this simple principle of communication: *Meanings are in people, not in words.*

### The Problem of Semantics

*Semantic problems* occur when people forget that a single word or expression may have different meanings. The semantic problems are further complicated by the fact that several different words may have the same meaning. For example, surely you can think of different words that mean the same as the three words listed below.[1]

1. Money _____ _____ _____
2. Home _____ _____ _____
3. Car _____ _____ _____

Every day people get into arguments because of misunderstandings over the meanings of words. A manager may tell an employee to do something that the employee seems to understand. Yet the employee may actually end up doing the wrong things because what he or she does is not what the manager intended to have done. Thus, a communication breakdown occurs that can cause serious human relations problems.

Ralph's mistake is an example of the problem of semantics. On Monday morning Ralph's manager called him into the office and said, "Ralph, last week's sales were terrible! In fact, sales for the entire month are 20 percent below last year at this time. The employees seem to spend more time in arguing with one another than in selling. I want you to find out what the trouble is and put an end to it. Do you understand?

"OK, boss," replied Ralph, who was the manager's assistant. "I'll take care of it."

On Tuesday morning two employees came up to the manager's office. They were extremely upset! Ralph had found out that these two employees were the cause of the many arguments that had been taking place. So, he fired them!

Ralph's boss could not believe what Ralph did. He meant for Ralph to straighten out the situation when he said, "I want you to find out what the trouble is and put an end to it." To Ralph, this meant an entirely different thing. The

[1]Money (capital, cash); home (apartment, condominium, house); car (wheels, transportation, automobile).

manager forgot that meanings are in people, not in words.

Communication problems that result from the problem of semantics can be avoided if the manager practices two important rules of communication. First, a manager must recognize that words by themselves have different meanings. Second, the manager must ask employees *what* they understood, not *if* they understood. Too many problems begin when a manager asks, "Do you understand?" or "Do you have any questions?" This question is not a good form of communication because any employee would be under pressure to answer, "Yes, I understand," even though he or she does not understand. In the case of Ralph, the communication problem could have been avoided if the manager had said, "Tell me what you understand," or "Tell me what you are going to do about it, Ralph." Surely it takes an extra minute to think about good communication, but the cost is small when compared to the cost of problems that arise when the right questions are not asked.

## The Problem of "Allness"

A manager or employee who believes that what she or he says is absolute, complete, certain, or final is guilty of *allness*. The tone of allness is suggested by the use of such words as *always, ever,* and *never*. This problem of allness is more common than one might think. It is illustrated in conversations that take place every day.

### *Oversimplification*

The problem of allness occurs because of the tendency to simplify things. A person makes things simple by reducing something large to something small. When something is small, it is easier to remember. To illustrate the process of oversimplification, let us take the example of a motorist who stops to ask a service station attendant for directions to a certain place.

**Motorist:** How do I get to Riverfront Stadium?

Illus. 6-4. The tone of allness is suggested by the use of the word *always.*

**Attendant:** Well, go down this street you're on for three blocks. Turn right at the four-way stop, then go to the second stoplight and turn left. It will be about a half mile on your right—you can't miss it.
**Motorist:** Let's see now, right at the four-way, two stops and a left, half mile right.

In this example, the motorist repeats the directions given by simplifying the main parts. The motorist does not repeat the full statement of directions.

### The "Sample of One" Judgment

When it comes to any business or employment conditions, however, oversimplification can result in an especially dangerous problem of allness. It can have a bad effect on human relations.

For example, Mrs. Marvin, the chief supervisor of a hospital, likes to talk with the employees from time to time. She walks through the food service area and talks to one employee. Then she walks around the second floor and talks with a nurse. Mrs. Marvin talks to another nurse on the third floor and does the same thing on the fourth and fifth floors. Finally she goes back to her office and thinks about the things that were said to her. She remembers the food service worker complaining about the part-time employees who were not taking work seriously. Mrs. Marvin also remembers that the nurse on the second floor complained about the janitors who were not cleaning the floors properly. Each of the nurses on the third, fourth, and fifth floors talked in very general terms, not saying much of anything.

Mrs. Marvin then concludes that things are going well on the third, fourth, and fifth floors. She also concludes that there are problems on the second floor and in food service. Therefore, at a later conference with the head of food service, Mrs. Marvin made the following remark: "I hear the part-time workers are not doing good work." The head of food service did not know what to say because Mrs. Marvin's statement was not absolutely true. Mrs. Marvin had talked with only one person, yet she made a judgment about the part-time workers. This was a *sample-of-one* judgment—a judgment based on a statement from only one person. Mrs. Marvin was not aware that she was making the judgment based on such little evidence. Her case is a classic example of the problem of allness—making a dangerous sample-of-one judgment without knowing what she was doing.

### Being Aware of Allness

To avoid allness at all times is impossible. People would almost have to stop talking if they had to think before uttering a single word. Nevertheless, one may make an effort to become more aware of allness. Here are three suggestions to help you:

1. As you read or listen, try to detect simplifications that others make. As you become sensitive to the process, you will become more aware of your own simplifications of thought.[2]
2. Make a habit of saying to yourself, "et cetera." It means "and so on and so forth." This will remind you that it is not possible to cover everything.[3]

[2]William Y. Haney, *Communication and Interpersonal Relations* (Homewood, Ill.: Richard D. Irwin, Inc., 1979), p. 359.
[3]*Ibid.*, p. 501.

3. Become sensitive to the words *always, never,* and *everything.* These words are indicators of allness.[4]

## Misuse of Language

Employers and employees can cause communication problems by misusing language. Two of the most serious communication problems that arise because of the misuse of language are (1) labeling, or name calling, and (2) emotional confusion.

### *Labeling, or Name Calling*

*Name calling,* or *labeling,* means to unfairly classify someone as a certain type of person. Typical labels given to people are:

1. Clown—a person who appears to do silly things on a regular basis.
2. Troublemaker—a person who appears to be frequently involved in controversy.
3. Animal—a person lacking in manners.

Labeling is a twofold human relations problem. That is, two things can happen when a person has been labeled: (1) the person will tend to *live up* to the label, or (2) the person will do dangerous things to *live down* the label.

***Living Up to a Label.*** Here is an example of a person who lives up to a label. Ben worked in a large office with about a hundred co-workers. On his first day in the office, Ben noticed that old screwdrivers and pliers were left in the desk he inherited. That very afternoon the tools came in handy. An employee's desk drawer was stuck and Ben fixed it.

Ben enjoyed being helpful. He soon earned the reputation of "Mr. Fixit." As time went by, Ben began volunteering to

Illus. 6-5. Labeling means to unfairly classify someone as a certain type of person.

[4]*Ibid.*, p. 502.

fix file cabinets, air-conditioning vents, and broken floor tiles, to mention only a few things. However, attempting to fix a telephone proved to be Ben's downfall. After "fiddling" with the telephone for a half hour, Ben accidentally dropped it on his toe. The telephone broke into a few large pieces and numerous small pieces.

The results of Ben's sincere effort to be helpful were surprising. Ben's co-worker, who relied on the telephone for a large volume of productivity, was unproductive for a day while waiting for a replacement phone. Ben had to be sent to the company medical department to have his toe checked. This resulted in several hours of lost productivity to Ben and some unnecessary medical paperwork for Ben's supervisor. Moreover, the company union was upset because Ben was doing "craft" work. This resulted in more lost hours of productivity because the union requested to meet with Ben's supervisor to discuss this small, but, to them, significant breach of the labor contract. Ben's efforts to live up to his label proved to be expensive!

***Living Down a Label.*** This example tells about a person who tries to live down a label. Jill's first week at her new job turned out to be unpleasant. She wanted to look nice, so she dressed up. Jill had her hair styled and really looked good. The trouble was she looked *too good.* No one said much to her that first week. On Friday some of her co-workers let her know that she was overdressed.

Although Jill got the message about being overdressed, it was too late. Her co-workers had begun to refer to her as "Miss Fashion." During her second week at work, Jill dressed like everyone else did. But the nickname Miss Fashion stuck, and Jill didn't like it. She therefore began to dress down by wearing sloppy clothes. That didn't work, and the nickname stayed with her. Jill continued to dress even more sloppily. Finally, Jill's supervisor had to talk to her about her careless, slovenly appearance. In her efforts to live down her label, Jill suffered some problems. She became upset with her co-workers, and her supervisor became upset with her.

## *Emotional Confusion*

Earlier in this chapter you learned that a word can have many different

Illus. 6-6. Jill tried to live down her label of "Miss Fashion."

meanings. You also learned that several words can mean the same thing.

***Use Pleasant-Sounding Words or Titles.*** Among words that mean the same thing, some have a pleasant sound while others do not. At work, especially, it is important to emphasize the positive side of things by using words that sound pleasant. For example, who would want to buy *death insurance?* Probably very few. However, *life insurance* is being sold to millions of people.

Would you prefer to buy luggage that is labeled "imitation leather" or "leatherette"? Both are the same. Grocery stores don't sell "hamburger"—they do sell "ground beef."

A group of words that also appeal to the emotions consists of ccupational titles. For example, which of the following titles would you prefer?

| Negative Appeal (-) | | Positive Appeal (+) |
|---|---|---|
| garbage collector | *or* | sanitation worker |
| shrink | *or* | psychologist |
| cop | *or* | police officer |
| disc jockey | *or* | radio personality |
| cook | *or* | chef |
| driver | *or* | chauffeur |

The words and occupational titles are not problems in themselves. They only serve to illustrate this point: *You can say things in a positive tone, and you can say the same things in a negative tone.*

***Watch Out for Emotionally Loaded Words.*** Emotional confusion results when people forget that some words have a negative appeal, or sound unpleasant to others. Such words are called *emotionally loaded words.* Some examples of emotionally loaded words and their positive counterparts follow:

| Emotionally Loaded Words | Less Emotionally Loaded Words |
|---|---|
| cheap | inexpensive |
| sick | ill |
| fired | asked to resign |
| worried | concerned |
| lie | not true |
| pop quiz | unscheduled test |

Although the emotionally loaded words listed above may sound all right to you, remember that to others these words may have a negative tone.

Forgetting that some words are emotionally loaded can cause a serious human relations problem. For example, one afternoon Mrs. Walton, general manager of the Central Lumber Company, walked out of her office to the cash register area. Three employees were standing by the register and talking. Mrs. Walton told the employees to stop gossiping and to straighten the counter displays. She did not think that the word *gossiping* was emotionally loaded, for she often used it. As a result, one of the employees became very upset. He was not a gossip, and he resented Mrs. Walton's use of this word. To this employee a gossip was a very crude and disgusting person.

Another example is Stan, an airline flight attendant, who forgot about emotionally loaded words. As the plane was flying into some stormy weather, Stan announced over the loud speakers: "We are approaching a *storm.* Please fasten your seat belts for your own safety." This announcement disturbed the passengers of Flight 106. Stan should have said: "We are approaching some turbulence. Please fasten your seat belts. You will be more comfortable."

***Avoid Sexist Language.*** A common misuse of language that results in human relations problems is sexist language. Such language indicates prejudicial discrimination against both men and women, but more often against women.

For example, a male manager wrote on the performance appraisal of a female subordinate: "friendly and bubbly." The term *bubbly*, although intended to be positive, is not a term generally attributable to *both* sexes. The manager was guilty of sexist language. He would have been better off using only the adjective "friendly."

Below is a list of sexist words that at one time were thought of as acceptable. To the right of each word is an appropriate term (nonsexist) for today's standards.

| Sexist | Nonsexist |
|---|---|
| foreman | supervisor |
| businessman | business executive |
| insurance man | insurance agent |
| chairman | chairperson |
| manpower | work force |
| mankind | humanity |
| Congressman | Representative |
| housewife | homemaker |
| usherette | usher |
| policeman | police officer |
| mailman | mail carrier |
| fireman | firefighter |

### *Tips on Avoiding the Misuse of Language*

It is possible to avoid communication problems caused by labeling and the use of emotionally loaded words. Here are some tips to help you:

1. Don't react to labels. If someone labels you, remember that the person is expressing an opinion. Everyone has a right to his or her opinion. You need not agree with it. Remember that there are many other people in your life who do not try to label you.
2. Avoid labeling others by practicing empathy. *Empathy* means seeing the world through the eyes of the other person. You would not like to be labeled. Don't label others.
3. Use positively loaded words to describe things. You will rarely offend someone by referring to the good side of things, people, or events.
4. Be constantly ready to explain your intentions. When someone reacts the opposite way from the way you thought the person would, stop talking and start explaining. The easiest way to do this is to say, "I didn't mean it that way, let me try again."

To summarize this section, remember that good communication will improve human relations. Sharing and understanding messages is only the beginning of good communication. Remember that meanings are in people, not in words. When you hear someone making absolute statements, be alert for communication problems. Watch out for labels and for emotionally loaded words. Good listening, which will be discussed in the next section of this chapter, will help you be aware of these things.

## THE IMPORTANCE OF GOOD LISTENING

Listening requires more than just hearing. This means that a good listener thinks about what is being said. When a good listener does not understand a message, he or she asks the speaker for a different explanation. A good listener must be alert. Listening is much more than hearing. The process of listening requires an active mind.

People at work spend more time in listening than in any other form of communication. Experts in communication generally agree that on a typical workday people spend the following amounts of time on the different forms of communication:

| | |
|---|---|
| Listening | 45 percent of the day |
| Speaking | 30 percent of the day |
| Reading | 15 percent of the day |
| Writing | 10 percent of the day |

Unfortunately, most people do not truly listen to what is being said. They may hear, but they do not listen. At work it is especially important to acquire the habit of good listening because good listening is good communication. And good communication promotes good human relations.

## Why People Don't Listen Well

There are three main reasons why people are poor listeners. These are (1) people think faster than they speak, (2) emotions block out certain messages, and (3) planning a reply gets in the way of listening.

Illus. 6-7. A good listener thinks about what is being said.

Illus. 6-8. The time gap between thinking and talking may result in a listening problem.

## People Think Faster Than They Speak

The human brain operates at an amazingly high speed. On the average, a person's brain can process 600 or 700 words a minute. Yet most people talk at a rate of about 125 words a minute. This time gap results in a listening problem. The brain finds it very easy to listen and, at the same time, to think other thoughts. When this happens, the mind begins to wander. As a result, listening is not consistent because people allow themselves to be distracted. This kind of listening is often covered up by pretending to listen when, in fact, the listener is thinking other thoughts.

## Emotions Block Out Some Messages

Emotions color one's understanding of what is being said. When a person is involved in a situation, he or she is likely to listen with bias. Certain signals can serve to warn you that emotions may be interfering with your listening. These signals are (1) when you resent the opposition and (2) when your personality clashes with the other speaker's personality.

***Resenting the Opposition.*** It is easy to listen to someone who agrees with you. However, it is more difficult to listen to someone with whom you do not agree.

For example, Earl has trouble listening to people who do not agree with him. He works at Building Supplies, a retail lumber and fixture store. Unfortunately, Earl loses a lot of customers because of his open resentment of any opposition to his ideas. For instance, when a customer wanted the B & B brand for a light switch, Earl said that the Levington brand was much better. When the customer preferred to buy the B & B brand, Earl got a little upset. As a result, the customer left the store while Earl went to the stockroom for the B & B switch. The customer did not wait for Earl to get the switch.

***Clashing Personalities.*** It is much easier to listen to someone you like. Listening to someone you don't like can be a problem. When we don't like the speaker, we tend to do one of four things:

1. We give attention to how the speaker is saying things and what items the speaker is emphasizing. Then we question whether we like the speaker's tone or emphasis.
2. We listen for areas of disagreement instead of agreement. When we hear something we disagree with, we "turn off" the message.
3. We allow the speaker's distracting habits or mannerisms to capture our attention.
4. We look at the way the speaker is dressed and find fault with it.

In short, we allow the speaker's personality to block the message.

A personality clash at work can sometimes result in a costly experience. For example, Roberta did not like Ricardo, her co-worker. One Monday morning Ricardo called the office to say that he would not be at work on time. It was Roberta who answered the phone. Ricardo explained why he would be late that day and then hung up. But Roberta did not really listen. All she heard Ricardo say was that he would not be in to work. At that point Roberta said to herself, "Well, good." Then Roberta reported to the supervisor that Ricardo called to say that he wouldn't be at work.

As a result of Roberta's inaccurate report, the supervisor had to call another employee, Sheila, to come to work. Although it was Sheila's day off, she agreed to work that day. When Sheila arrived at the office, however, she found Ricardo just arriving, too. Of course, Sheila became angry, but the supervisor was even angrier! Roberta had caused a lot of trouble and expense because she did not listen carefully to Ricardo, whom she disliked.

### *Planning a Reply Hinders Good Listening*

A true conversation between two people rarely occurs. Supposedly, when two people have a conversation, one talks and the other listens. However, more often this is not the case. Most people simply do not listen to what is being said. Actually they listen for a moment of silence that will allow them to speak.

Illus. 6-9. Do you listen or do you think about what you are going to say?

For example, as one person begins to tell about a recent activity, the other person begins to think of one of his or her own recent experiences. When the speaker pauses—and this is that moment of silence—the other person jumps into the conversation with his or her own story. Rarely does the listener respond directly to what the speaker has just said. Instead, the listener begins to talk about what he or she was thinking.

Simply listening for the moment of silence creates a communication problem. In the dialogue given below, notice how no one responds to what was first said. Each speaker tells a related story, but the attempt to get a real conversation going *is* frustrated!

**Rob:** I saw a terrific horror film on the late show last night. . . .
**Mike:** Oh, did you sec the one a week ago Friday night about Dracula?
**Lany:** Hey, don't you people ever sleep? I was so tired last night. I worked until midnight and then went straight home. . . .
**Rob:** This one last night started about midnight, a good science fiction movie. The earth was about to explode. . . .

## What Good Listening Requires

Effective listening requires two skills. These are (1) the ability to listen for facts and (2) the ability to listen for feelings.

### *Ability to Listen for Facts*

Listening for facts comes more naturally than listening for feelings. Most people try to get the facts while listening and are able to respond to facts. Illus. 6-11 contains some statements made by a worker. What facts can you find in the worker's message?

Illus. 6-10. Listen for facts and for feelings.

## Facts in the Message

______________________________

______________________________

______________________________

Obviously the fact in the worker's message is this: The heating system does not work. If a listener's answer is based on facts only, that answer would probably be as follows: "Okay, I'll tell the boss and we'll do something about the heating system."

## Ability to Listen for Feelings

It is important to let a person know that you're listening for his or her feelings. When a person expresses any feelings, that person wants the listener to know about the feelings that are expressed.

Look at Illus. 6-11 again. What feelings are expressed in the worker's message?

## Feelings in the Message

______________________________

______________________________

______________________________

The feelings expressed by the worker could range anywhere from anger to humor. If the worker is serious, she is probably expressing any or all of the following feelings:

Illus. 6-11. What are the facts in the message?

1. She is angry about the heating system not working.
2. She is angry at the boss.
3. She is concerned about being cold while working.

If the listener's answer is based on both facts and feelings, that answer would probably be as follows: "The heating system doesn't work, huh? No wonder you're upset. I'll tell the boss, and we'll do something about it. I know she would not want you to work in a cold room."

When a person's expressed feelings are ignored the first time around, that person will usually make a second attempt to express feelings. The dialogue given below is an example.

> **Employee:** Where in the world is Charlie? I've got a report to do. He has the books locked in his desk. He's never around when you need him.
> **Manager:** I'll use my key to open his desk and get the books. Then you can get your report finished.
> **Employee:** Don't bother. We'll never find the right accounts in his messy desk. If you were more strict, he'd be here. This office is the most disorganized place I've ever seen.

In the example just given, the manager failed to listen for feelings in the employee's first outburst. The second outburst of emotion could have been prevented if the manager had responded to the facts and feelings as follows: "I don't know where Charlie is. It sounds like you're upset because he should have given you the books before he left. Would it help if I unlocked the desk with my key?"

The greatest thing about responding to facts and feelings is that is works! Try it. Remember to listen for feelings. Let the person know that you are listening to feelings that are being expressed. You will be pleased with the results.

## How to Improve Listening Habits

Good listening habits will improve human relations. By listening to others carefully, you silently tell them you care about what they have to say. Here are some tips to help you improve listening:

1. Encourage others to talk. As you encourage others to speak, you feel more responsible for listening. You also learn from and about others when they talk.
2. Use nonverbal actions to encourage the person who is talking. Look at the person while he or she is talking; nod as you hear the meaning of what is being said; say uh-huh and hmm. These actions tell the person that you are listening.
3. Take advantage of your fast-working mind. Remember people can only speak about 125 words per minute. Your mind can process five times as much in the same time period. Use the extra time to repeat and rephrase what the person is saying.
4. When your mind wanders, admit it—at least to yourself. Then ask the speaker to repeat what was said.
5. Don't interrupt. Interrupting someone can cause hard feelings. Remember you are not on a quiz show. You need not blurt out an answer before the speaker has finished.
6. Prevent emotional deafness. When you sense that you are getting angry because of the speaker's message, take positive action. Avoid negative action such as turning off the message. Use your emotions for fine-tuning. Listen for assump-

tions and for the logic in what is being said.

7. Listen for feelings as well as for facts. Listening for facts is more natural than listening for feelings. Most people can get the facts in a message. Listening for a person's feelings is difficult. By listening for feelings, you improve listening in two ways. First, you will become more aware of your own emotions. When you are aware of your own emotions, you can control them. Second, as you listen for feelings, you will have a better understanding of what the speaker really means.

## OFFICIAL AND UNOFFICIAL COMMUNICATION

Most people recognize that there are two systems of communication that exist at work: (1) the formal system and (2) the informal system. Communication at work can therefore be official (formal) or unofficial (informal), depending on which type of organization is used to relay the communication.

### Formal Organization for Official Communication

The formal system of organization allows work to be done quickly and smoothly. This system is the official way of dividing the work among all employees. It is also a way of dividing authority and responsibility among the managers and supervisors. A *formal organization* is usually illustrated by means of an organization chart. Illus. 6-12 shows the organization chart of a department store.

An organization chart represents the official chain of command at work. It shows the official (1) lines of authority, (2) areas of responsibility, and (3) lines of communication.

#### *Lines of Authority*

*Authority* is the power or right to command or lead. It is possible to tell who has authority by looking at an organization chart from top to bottom. In Illus. 6-12, the first position of authority is held by the store manager, who is at the top. The store manager has authority over all employees. The second position of authority is shared by five people. They are the personnel manager, the advertising manager, the sales manager, the finance manager, and the maintenance manager. The merchandise buyers are in the third position of authority. Each of these buyers reports to the sales manager. Next in line are the department managers, who have less authority than the merchandise buyers. At the bottom of the chart are the salespeople. As you can see, the salespersons have no authority over anyone in the store.

#### *Areas of Responsibility*

*Responsibility* means that a person must answer or account for what happens. It means accepting blame for failure or accepting credit for success. The more things or people you must answer for, the greater are your chances of success as well as failure.

The areas of responsibility for all employees are also shown on an organization chart. Illus. 6-12 shows that the store manager is responsible for the entire store. The sales manager is responsible for all the employees and business transactions in the sales division. The mer-

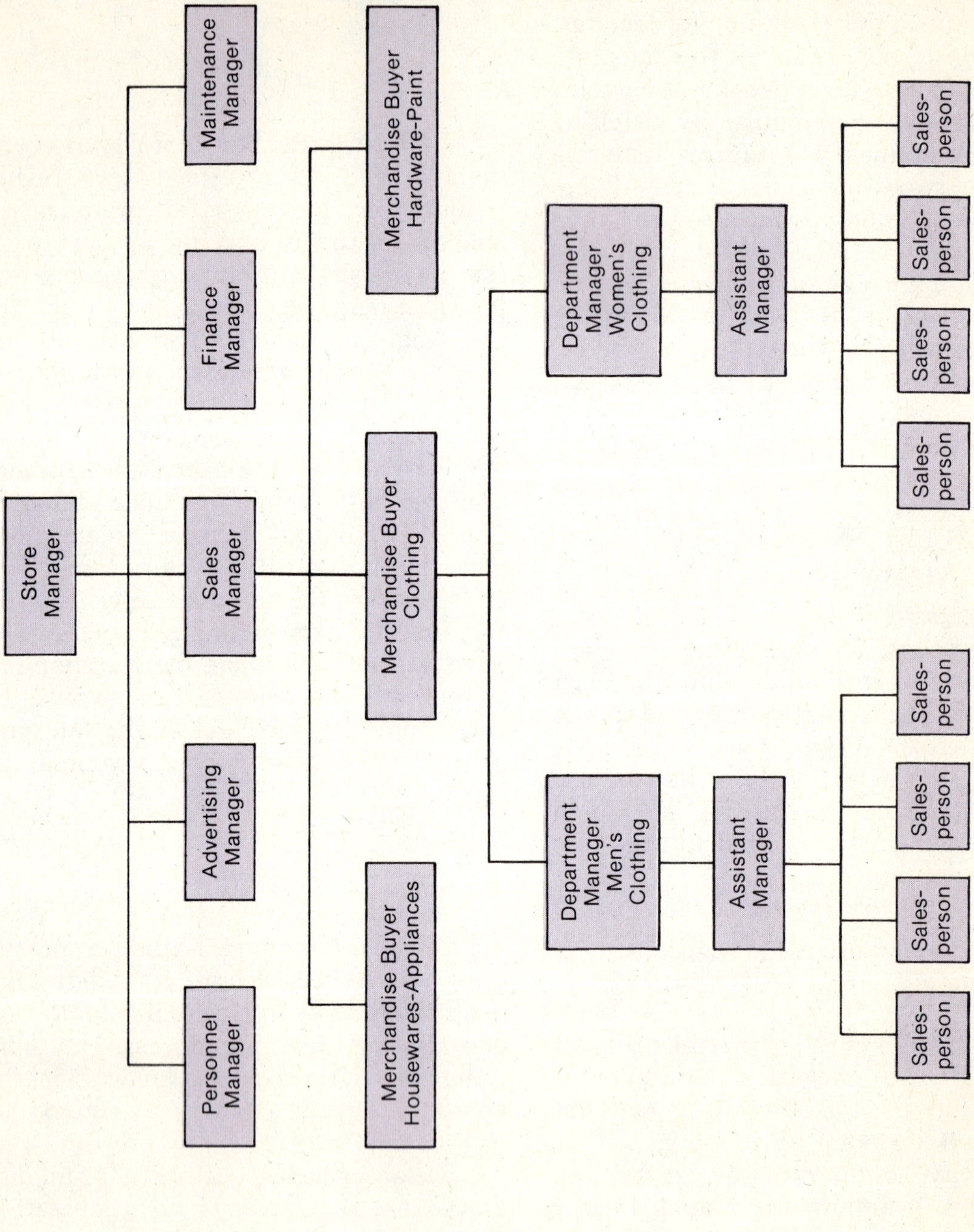


Illus. 6-12. Organization chart of a department store.

chandise buyers help the sales manager purchase merchandise. The merchandise buyer for clothing is responsible for both the Men's Clothing Department and the Women's Clothing Department. Each department manager is responsible for everything that takes place in the department. The assistant managers help the department managers in two ways: They help keep inventories of the clothing merchandise and help in supervising the salesperson.

Illus. 6-13 shows an upside-down triangle that indicates the amount of authority and responsibility held by people in an organization. The small area at the lower tip of the triangle represents a small amount of authority and responsibility. Notice that the area becomes larger as it goes further up from the tip. This means that people higher up in the organization have larger amounts of authority and responsibility.

## *Lines of Communication*

In the formal organization, lines of communication follow the lines on the organizational chart. For example, if the store manager in Illus. 6-12 decides to

Illus. 6-13. People higher up in an organization have larger amounts of authority and responsibility.

make a change in sales policy, notice of the policy change will *flow down.* In other words, official communication comes to an employee from his or her immediate supervisor.

Official communication from the top includes messages about the following matters:

1. Changes in company policy.
2. Hiring of a new employee.
3. Termination or transfer of employees.
4. Working hours.
5. Working schedules.
6. Sales goals.
7. Employee evaluations.
8. Pay raises and promotions.

It is possible that some co-workers may tell you about *this* or *that* communication. Until you hear the message from a supervisor or see it in writing, the communication is not official.

Official communications also *flow upward.* For example, a salesperson might have an idea on how to design a sales window display. The idea would be officially communicated upward, beginning with the salesperson's immediate supervisor. The salesperson does not go directly to the department manager or others higher in command. This would break the flow of communication and could result in leaving out important persons. The upward flow, like the downward flow, should be taken step by step.

## Informal Organization for Unofficial Communication

The *informal organization* refers to different groups at work that may be established because the members of these groups have something in common. For example, the members of a group may

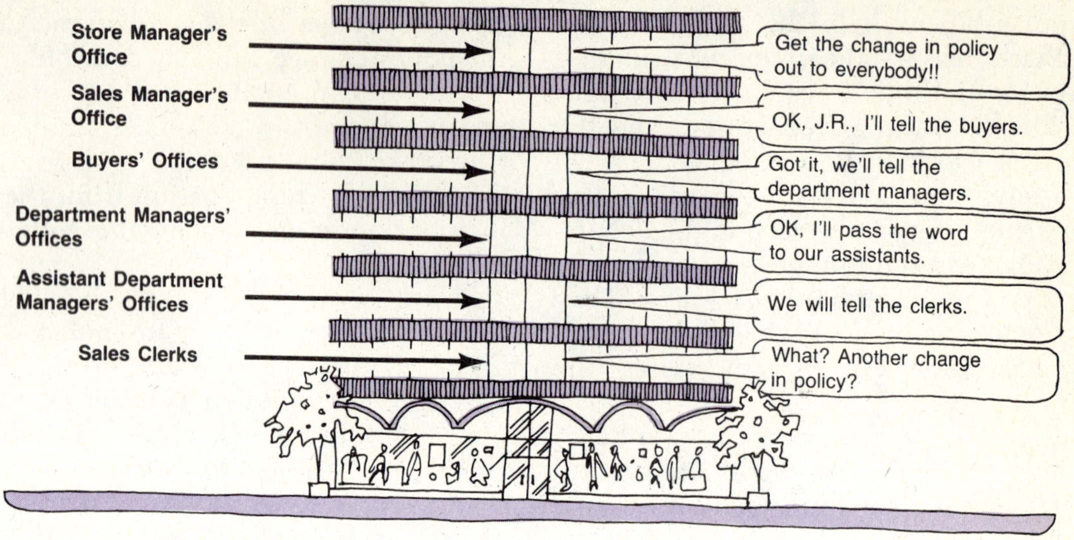


Illus. 6-14. Downward lines of communication.

Illus. 6-15. Upward flow of communication.

have a common social background, be of the same age bracket, have the same religion. These informal groups do not have formal authority. Yet the informal organization composed of these groups provides a system of informal communication. And sometimes this informal system may work more effectively than the formal one.

### *The Grapevine*

The unofficial system of communication provided by informal groups is known as the *grapevine.* The term grapevine dates back to the Civil War in the United States. At that time secret messages were sent over a telegraph line. This line was strung through trees and

Illus. 6-16. The grapevine.

bushes almost like a vine. Today, the term *grapevine* includes all forms of unofficial communication.

Unlike official communication, messages on the grapevine do not follow the lines on the organization chart. Illus. 6-17 shows a partial organization chart. The solid lines represent the official lines of communication. The broken lines represent the path taken by unofficial communication. Look at this chart and the unofficial lines of communication, and then read the next paragraph, which explains what took place.

Ruth overheard the store manager and the sales manager talking about changing the store hours. The store manager was thinking of keeping the store open until 9 p.m. on Thursday evenings. Then Ruth told Jake what she overheard. During lunch, Jake passed the same message to Lynn. Lynn then told all the other salespersons in the women's clothing department about it. As a result, Wally asked Linda if he had to work on Thursday night. But Linda didn't know what to say, for she had never heard of the change in store hours.

### *Is the Grapevine Accurate?*

Those who conduct studies about informal communication suggest that the grapevine is about 80 percent accurate. This means that most messages passed along the grapevine are almost right. The problem is, which of the parts of the message are right and which parts are wrong? One small change in a message can alter the meaning of the entire message. Serious human relations problems begin when people assume that the grapevine is 100 percent right.

For example, let us take the case of Dean, an employee in a store. During an afternoon break, the store manager's secretary told Dean that the store would be closed tomorrow in order to hold the store's annual inventory. Last year the store was closed for a half day so that the employees could take inventory of the goods. During the past two weeks, everyone at the store had been talking about the annual inventory. Dean was looking forward to that day because he could count the goods much more easily when

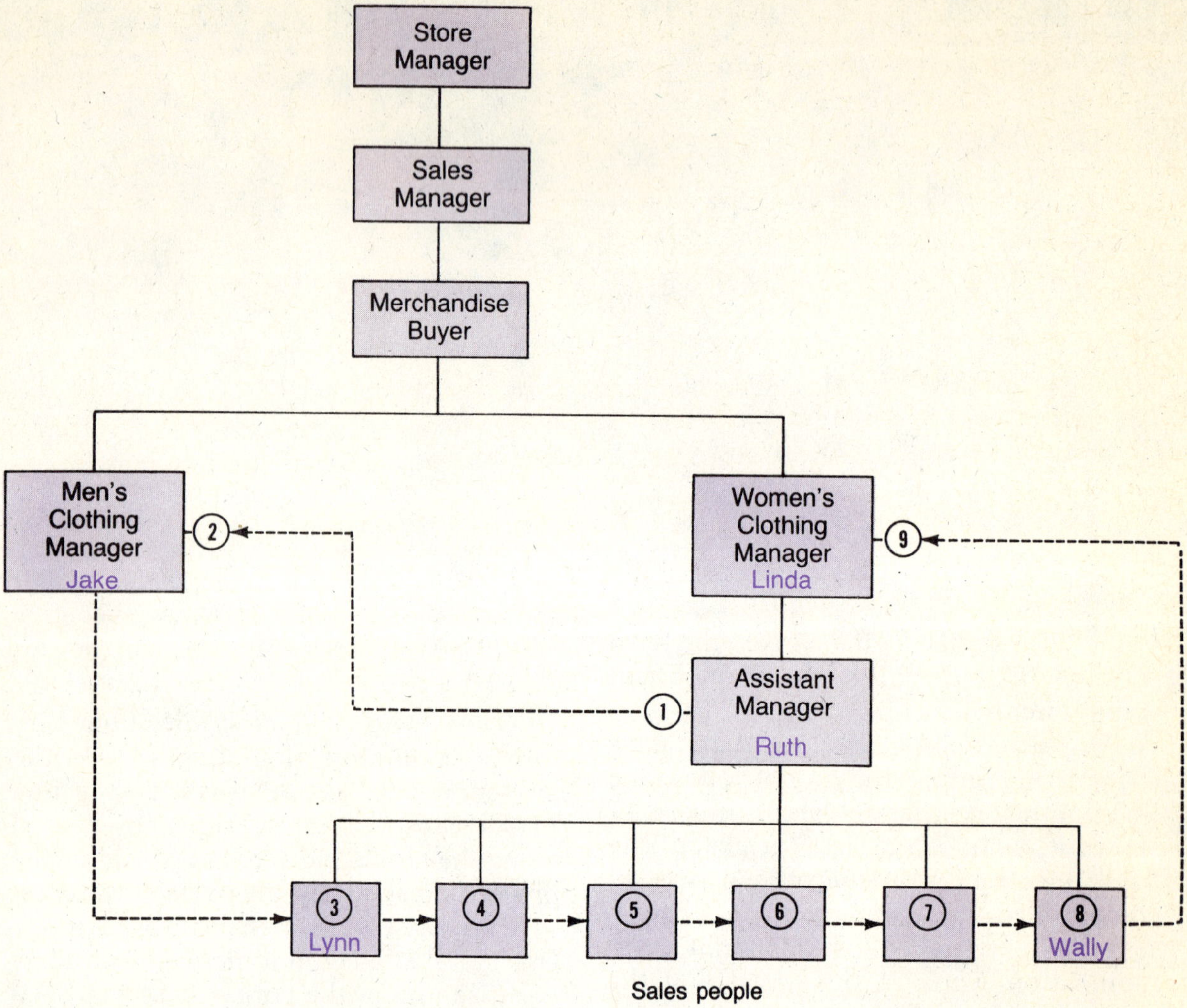


Illus. 6-17. The grapevine does not take the path taken by official communication.

he did not have to wait on customers. After his break, Dean told two of his co-workers to come to work tomorrow ready to take inventory. He simply told them what the store manager's secretary had said.

The next morning Dean and his two co-workers arrived at the store ready to take the inventory. They were all dressed casually for this purpose. On regular workdays they wore dress shirts and neckties. To their surprise, however, Dean and his co-workers found out that the store inventory would be taken that evening! Dean and his co-workers had to go home and change clothes.

Dean felt terrible, of course. He had caused problems for his two co-workers. Like Dean, they had to drive back home to change clothes. This took time and wasted energy. And Dean felt that he got them in trouble with the store manager. Naturally his co-workers were upset. The store manager was also upset because the store lost the sales that the employees would have made during the hour they were gone. Dean had created a human relations problem by assuming that the grapevine message he heard was accurate. The truth is, the store manager's secretary omitted one small important detail from this message: *the taking of inventory was to be held at night.* Thus, her message was not complete. The secretary's message was only 80 percent right; 20 percent of the message was left out!

### *How Do Rumors Spread?*

The grapevine sometimes has a bad reputation because it can spread rumors. A rumor is a widely spread story based on incomplete information. Some rumors may be true, and some may be false.

Rumors can be described by the following formula:

$$\text{Rumor} = \text{Interest} \times \text{Clarity}$$

This formula states that a rumor depends on two factors: interest and clarity. The first factor has to do with the amount of interest a person has in the rumor. For example, a rumor about an employee marrying the boss might be of great interest to some employees, but not to others. A rumor about an employee getting fired may be of less interest to some than others. The right combination of interest and fuzzy details will provide a rumor.

The second factor in the formula is clarity. This means that the more confusing a message is, the more likely a rumor will result. For example, a story about an employee getting a traffic ticket for speeding could easily become a rumor. All it takes is for one person to tell the story with a few fuzzy details, as illustrated in the dialogue below. Note how the lack of clear information adds to the rumor.

**Bob to Sally:** George got a ticket for speeding.
**Sally to Harry:** George was arrested for speeding.
**Harry to Joan:** The police got George for speeding.
**Joan to Susan:** I knew George would get in trouble; now he's in jail.

Rumors, like other messages on the grapevine, are about 80 percent accurate. However, if the message is highly emotional, its accuracy goes down. For example, a rumor that the boss is being transferred may be slightly emotional, but the rumor that the boss's replacement is big, tough, and mean could be very emotional. Scare stories about the new boss could spread quickly.

In summary, informal communication occurs every day. One cannot depend on messages from the grapevine to be accurate. Whenever possible, you should ask your supervisor about the accuracy of an informal message. The grapevine also carries rumors. Rumors are probably not true if the messages they carry are emotionally loaded. By understanding the limitations of informal communication, you will improve human relations at work.

# Activity 6-1

## Understanding the Definition of *Communication*

The following projects will help you understand the first section of this chapter, "Definition of *Communication*"

1. Bring to class examples of the following:

   a. A company magazine. What kind of information does the magazine communicate?
   b. A company newsletter. What kind of information does the newsletter contain?

2. Interview three people by asking them this question: "How do you define good communication?" Write their answers in the spaces provided below. Then share your findings with the class.

### Interviewee 1

______________________________

______________________________

______________________________

### Interviewee 2

______________________________

______________________________

______________________________

### Interviewee 3

______________________________

______________________________

______________________________

3. Draw a model on the next page to illustrate the communication process. Use the model on page 192 in this chapter to help you get started. Try to include barriers to communication in your model.

4. Look up in a dictionary the words listed below. Then count the number of different meanings given for each word. Also indicate the most common meaning of each word.

| Word | Number of Meanings | Most Common Meaning of the Word |
|---|---|---|
| run | ________ | ____________________ |
| capital | ________ | ____________________ |
| common | ________ | ____________________ |
| tone | ________ | ____________________ |
| part | ________ | ____________________ |

# Activity 6-2

## Meanings Are in People, Not in Words

This activity will help you understand why meanings are in people and not in words.

On the next page, write a story about a communication problem at school. Follow these directions carefully.

1. Notice that the next page has 25 lines on it. You begin the story by writing a sentence or part of a sentence on Line 1. Do not write on Line 2.
2. Tear out the page and give it to another person in the class, Person 2. The sentence written by Person 2 should continue the story you began.
3. Person 2 must now fold the paper so that the sentence you wrote on Line 1 cannot be seen.
4. Person 2 should give the paper to Person 3.
5. Person 3 reads only the sentence written by Person 2. Then Person 3 writes on Line 3.
6. Person 3 must now fold the paper so that Lines 1 and 2 cannot be seen. Person 3 passes the paper to Person 4.
7. Person 4 may only read the sentence or words written on Line 3.
8. Other persons in the class should continue adding lines to the story in the same manner. Be sure that the paper is folded so that the next writer sees only the previous line.
9. After everyone in the class has written a line, read the story.
10. Was the story funny? How does the story illustrate the point that meanings are in people, not in words?

1. ______________________________
2. ______________________________
3. ______________________________
4. ______________________________
5. ______________________________
6. ______________________________
7. ______________________________
8. ______________________________
9. ______________________________
10. ______________________________
11. ______________________________
12. ______________________________
13. ______________________________
14. ______________________________
15. ______________________________
16. ______________________________
17. ______________________________
18. ______________________________
19. ______________________________
20. ______________________________
21. ______________________________
22. ______________________________
23. ______________________________
24. ______________________________
25. ______________________________

# Activity 6-3

## Understanding What Allness Is

Your teacher will need several volunteers for this activity. If you do not choose to be a volunteer, you must complete the "observer" part of this activity.

This activity requires that you listen carefully. When you have completed this activity, you will have a better understanding of allness. Follow these directions carefully.

### To the Volunteers

Form a circle with your desks in the center of the room., The teacher will give each of you an envelope. Open your envelope and read the directions in it. After you have read the directions, begin your discussion.

### To the Observers

You have a special job during this activity. You must take notes about the discussion. Use the next page to write your notes. Listen for allness statements that the role-players make. When you hear words like *always, never,* and *every time,* write what was said on the note page. Remember that allness statements are not limited to the three words mentioned above.

## NOTE PAGE ON ALLNESS STATEMENTS

Allness Statements by Volunteer 1

Allness Statements by Volunteer 2

Allness Statements by Volunteer 3

Allness Statements by Volunteer 4

Allness Statements by Volunteer 5

Allness Statements by Volunteer 6

# Activity 6-4

## Listening for Emotionally Loaded Words

Two student volunteers are needed for this activity. One student will role-play a company manager. The other student will role-play an employee. By completing this activity you will learn about the dangers of emotionally loaded words.

### Role of Manager

You are the manager of Company Z. You must discipline an employee who came to work late for the third time. The employee also dresses inappropriately. This carelessness hurts the company. Use emotionally loaded words as you talk to the employee.

### Role of Employee

You are to react to the manager as you think the employee would react. Disagree and show signs of tension.

The time allowed for this activity is five minutes. The teacher will, if possible, tape record the conversation. After the conversation, the teacher will play back the tape. The tape will be stopped every few sentences so that everyone can list the emotionally loaded words or sentences in the conversation. Use the next page to write your list.

After the taped conversation ends, write a *less* emotionally worded script of the conversation opposite the emotionally loaded script in your list. Then answer the following questions:

1. How did the employee react to the emotionally loaded words? Describe the employee's reaction.

______________________________________

______________________________________

2. Explain the difference between a positive tone and a negative tone. Which do you prefer?

______________________________________

______________________________________

3. Is a negative approach ever justified? When?

______________________________________

______________________________________

4. Did you hear any statements of allness? If so, what were the statements?

______________________________________

______________________________________

5. Did labeling occur? If so, give examples.

______________________________________

______________________________________

6. List two ways to avoid emotionally loaded words. How can you apply the two ways to the discussion between the manager and the employee?

______________________________________

______________________________________

______________________________________

______________________________________

| Emotionally Loaded Words or Sentences | A Better Way to Say the Message |
|---|---|
| | |
| | |
| | |
| | |
| | |
| | |
| | |
| | |
| | |
| | |

# Activity 6-5

## Listening for Facts and Feelings

This activity will help you learn to listen for feelings as well as facts. Remember that most people can get the facts in a message. It is more difficult to listen for feelings. Keep this formula in mind as you take part in this activity.

Message = Facts and Feelings

Four student volunteers are needed to put on a demonstration debate for the class. Two student volunteers will support the issue, and the other two will oppose it. Each pair of debaters will attempt to influence the class to either agree or disagree with the following statement:

*Anyone who works hard for a living should be required to support others who fail to provide for themselves.*

The class may think of other issues to debate, but the one selected should contain a judgment based on feelings and opinions.

### To the Volunteer Debaters

Each debater has two minutes to argue for or against the issue. Try to separate fact from opinion. Use both logic and emotion to support your points. Follow this schedule for your debate:

| Speaker | Purpose |
|---|---|
| 1 | support |
| 2 | oppose |
| 3 | support |
| 4 | oppose |

After the debate is concluded, the audience should be polled to see how many agree and how many disagree with the issue debated. The class will be asked to explain why they voted as they did.

1. What problems come up when the opposing side forgets to listen for feelings?

______________________________

______________________________

______________________________

______________________________

2. Why is it difficult to get agreement on value statements?

______________________________

______________________________

______________________________

______________________________

3. How often did the opposing side mistake feelings for fact?

______________________________

4. Why is it more difficult to find proof for value statements than for statements of fact?

______________________________

______________________________

______________________________

______________________________

5. What communication barriers arise when false opinions and feelings get in the way of listening?

6. Did the audience let their own sentiments and attitudes affect the way they *heard* the arguments?

# Activity 6-6

## Case Study: The Wrong Time to Complain

This activity is designed to help you study the formal organization. By completing this activity, you will learn how to communicate effectively through the formal organization.

Chad was very happy on Tuesday morning. He went on his morning break with Charlie, the supervisor of the furniture department. Chad wanted to get transferred to the furniture department. While the two were drinking their coffee, Mr. Barnes, the store manager, sitting at a nearby table, called out: "Come over here, Charlie, I want to talk with you." Charlie then said, "Come on, Chad, let's go sit with the boss."

Chad sat quietly while Charlie and the store manager talked. After about five minutes, Chad decided to get into the conversation. Chad said, "You know, Mr. Barnes, I sure would like to sell furniture. I think I could sell furniture. At least I could sell it better than I sell those stupid toys!" Charlie then said, "Well, Chad, we'll talk about it." Chad replied, "Yes, I sure would like to talk about it."

Chad never did get his transfer. Can you figure out why he didn't?

1. Why did Charlie seem to avoid further talk about Chad's desire to be transferred?

______________________________

______________________________

______________________________

2. What do you think Mr. Barnes thought about Chad's actions?

______________________________

______________________________

______________________________

3. What is the proper way to apply for a transfer to another department? Use the organization chart shown on page 188 in the text to help you answer this question.

______________________________

______________________________

______________________________

# Activity 6-7

## Choosing Alternatives for Sexist Language

Below is a list of words and phrases. Select the words that are "sexist" and write the reason why the word or phrase is prejudicial. Then write an alternative word or phrase that is nonsexist.

*Example:* The phrase "career woman" is sexist because we do not refer to men as "career men." In our culture men are assumed to be in a career. An alternative word or phrase is "professional." Or simply name the woman's profession, as, for example, she is a "physician."

| Sexist Language[5] | Reason Why It Is Prejudicial | Alternative Word or Phrase |
|---|---|---|
| anchorman | ____________________ | ____________________ |
| draftsman | ____________________ | ____________________ |
| female lawyer | ____________________ | ____________________ |
| fisherman | ____________________ | ____________________ |
| manhole cover | ____________________ | ____________________ |
| male nurse | ____________________ | ____________________ |
| manicurist | ____________________ | ____________________ |
| repairman | ____________________ | ____________________ |
| secretary | ____________________ | ____________________ |
| stewardess | ____________________ | ____________________ |

[5] Hint: Some words in this list may *not* be prejudicial.

# Index